Generation Zion

Generation Zion, Volume 1

Dennis Grimes

Published by Dennis Grimes, 2024.

While every precaution has been taken in the preparation of this book, the publisher assumes no responsibility for errors or omissions, or for damages resulting from the use of the information contained herein.

GENERATION ZION

First edition. February 21, 2024.

Copyright © 2024 Dennis Grimes.

ISBN: 979-8224578672

Written by Dennis Grimes.

Table of Contents

Generation Zion 1

PART I – WHAT IS GENERATION ZION? 3

Chapter 1: THE GENERATION ZION CALLING AND DEFINITION 5

Chapter 2: THE GENERATION ZION PREPARATION 13

Chapter 3: THE GENERATION ZION AGAPAO! (UNCONDITIONAL LOVE IN ACTION) 39

Part II – THE GENERATION ZION WARRIOR PRIESTHOOD OF RAINBOW LIGHT 45

Chapter 4: TO "EN Dü O" (PUT ON) 47

Chapter 5: THE WARRIOR PRIESTHOOD 51

Chapter 6: THE GARMENT OF RAINBOW LIGHT 55

Chapter 7: THE PURPOSE OF THE GARMENT OF RAINBOW LIGHT 57

Chapter 8: THE GARMENT OF RAINBOW LIGHT: THE COLOR WHITE 63

Chapter 9: THE GARMENT OF RAINBOW LIGHT: THE COLOR RED 71

Chapter 10: THE GARMENT OF RAINBOW LIGHT: THE COLOR ORANGE 75

Chapter 11: THE GARMENT OF RAINBOW LIGHT: The Color Yellow 77

Chapter 12: THE GARMENT OF RAINBOW LIGHT: THE COLOR GREEN 81

Chapter 13: THE GARMENT OF RAINBOW LIGHT: THE COLOR BLUE 87

Chapter 14: THE GARMENT OF RAINBOW LIGHT: THE COLOR INDIGO 93

Chapter 15: THE GARMENT OF RAINBOW LIGHT: THE COLOR PURPLE 95

Part III – THE WARFARE OF "AGAPAO" (UNCONDITIONAL LOVE IN ACTION) 99

Chapter 16: FIGHTING FROM A SEATED POSITION 101

Chapter 17: THE MULTI-DIRECTIONAL DIMENSION OF PRAYER... 111

Chapter 18: THE CO-LABORING SUNG PRAYERS OF SAINTS AND ANGELS 117

ENDNOTES 129

This book is dedicated first to my Heavenly Father, to my Lord Jesus Christ, the Anointed One of Israel, and the Holy Spirit, for without His constant illumination and revelational knowledge of what the Father and Son are sovereignly doing in these last days, this book would never have been written. In addition, I would also dedicate this book to the sons and daughters of God that arise and walk-in full power with the fullness of the Holy Spirit.

I would also like to dedicate this book to my family, that has given me the time to study, pray, and seek God's direction for the writing of this book. First to my darling and beloved queen and wife Faith, my modern-day knight and son Eadward, and my princess, Sharlotte. "Poppa" Daniel Warner is the last person who helped me keep the flames alive on this book and persevere in finishing it up.

PART I – WHAT IS GENERATION ZION?

Chapter 1: THE GENERATION ZION CALLING AND DEFINITION

I want to encourage you that the change within the Body of Christ is here. It is time to lay down our own thoughts, prejudices, man-made rules, false-religiousness, self-destructive and sacrilegious attitudes, hidden agendas, unbecoming rituals, and pride in order to preach the gospel of the kingdom...as a witness to all the nations (Mat. 24:14 New King James Version (NKJV)). This emerging revolution and awakening are needed to prepare the way for the King of kings, Lord of Lords, and Almighty God.

THE CALL OF GENERATION ZION

On February 22, 2003, Dr. C. Peter Wagner, during "The Call Los Angeles" at the Rose Bowl Stadium in Pasadena, CA, declared and mandated a call for the new generation to arise and take their place and their authority as the new emerging apostles and prophets called Generation "Z" for Ground Zero. However, I would redefine it as Generation Zion for "Zero-Tolerance in Love."

These apostles and prophets will bring order and stand complete in Christ as He unleashes His ministries in full force which include the five-fold ministers. The five-fold ministries of Christ are the apostles, prophets, evangelists, pastors, and teachers. I want to elaborate on that, stating that it is time for the new wine to fill the new wineskins as part of this new generation.

WHY GENERATION ZION?

This generation will have the Spirit's word in their mouths and are covered with the shadow of the hand of God calling out those that are of Zion "HIS PEOPLE" (see Isa. 51:16). His people in Obadiah verse 21 (King James Version (KJV)) are described as the saviours who come up on mount Zion to judge the mount of Esau; and the kingdom shall be the Lord's. The saviours in this verse describe the Church judging Esau or the house of the flesh.

Galatians 5:19-21 (World English Bible (WEB)) describes the house of the flesh or works consisting of "sexual immorality, uncleanness, lustfulness,idolatry, sorcery, hatred, strife, jealousies, outbursts of anger, rivalries, divisions, heresies,envy, murders, drunkenness, orgies, and things like these... that those who practice such things will not inherit God's Kingdom."

With the above works of the flesh we as Christians see them in action at the public-school systems having instituted a code of ethics and rules known as zero-tolerance against speech, guns, drugs, gang symbols, personal attire, conduct, cleanliness, transgender, etc. which is hypocritical.

THE HYPOCRITCAL JUDGMENT

The Church judges the apostles and prophets because of the message of unbelief within Christendom that they have been reinstated. The way the Church keeps watch for the counterfeit prophets/apostles, miracle workers, and other independent ministries that walk according to My love and Spirit is the same way they judge the real apostle and prophets as if they are counterfeits without a code of conduct made up of zero-tolerance in love. The hypocritical aspect is that they are afraid of change and that they are old wineskins.

The old wineskins are the cold and lukewarm churches that have become full of religion, pride, and arrogance. They judge by the person's appearance and not loving them with the unconditional love of Christ. "For man looks at the outward appearance, but Yahweh looks at the heart" (1 Sam. 16:7 NKJV). Their wineskins have become old because they do not allow God to move due to human traditions built into the individual church. Thus, they cannot possess and hold the new wine that is being poured out by the quintillions of gallons upon the body of Christ.

THE GENERATION ZION ARMY

God is building up an army that is completely sold out to Him. They will not be filled with greed, envy, and strife but only with the Fear of the Lord and the love of Christ. This heavenly company wrapped in Earthly bodies will have mantles upon them that have not been seen since the first apostolic age of the Church, and I declare that we have entered the last apostolic age. The last apostolic age will culminate all the incredible dynamics of church history built into one generation with the entire portion of the **Spirit without Measure** (see John 3:34). The restructuring of Church government is at hand with an increase of an original Biblical theology that does not have any prejudice or racist thoughts conceived in it. This army will be the "Joel II Army of the Lord" focusing on the prophetic words of the Lord. We will hold fasts to prepare for war with the result of having entire cities saved. The holding of the fast in Joel 2 was for a mighty move of the Spirit to pour out on all flesh (see Joel 2:28), which was first fulfilled in Acts 2 as a model for that expectation for every city in the world.

THE THIRD DAY WINE

With this in mind, the Holy Spirit has saved the best for last. In past times, the armies of faithful men and women are the foundations upon which the Generation Zion army will march the Church triumphantly into the end of the age. It is the past movements that help culminate "the harvest."

During the wedding feast in Cana of Galilee, when Jesus turned the water into wine, and the master of the feast said, "everyone serves the good wine first, and when the guests have drunk freely, then that which is worse. You have kept the good wine until now," (John 2:10). God is giving His good or what should be considered the **best** wine now! Now, meaning currently, as you read this, He is filling you with His wine, which is the power of the Holy Spirit and the glory of the Father and Jesus that has not been tasted yet. What you taste now has not been tasted in the past. I would consider that the inferior wine. The wine today must and will have new wineskins. The rising army will be the new wineskins making the body a perfect man (see Eph. 4:13) being filled from the inside out with His best wine.

Also notable in this passage is verse 1, which proclaims that Jesus manifested this miracle on the third day of the wedding. Let me reveal to you that this was also a sign for today's emerging Church that the wine that we taste in this very hour is third-day wine. It was symbolic of Christ's resurrection on the third day, in which He would come out of the grave with the blessing of the Father and with renewed power from the Holy Spirit.

When you drink, drink long, drink far, drink wide, and drink deep. Drink until you cannot drink anymore, and then drink a little longer to be in overflow mode. To drink is to have communion with God. For as you eat the Bread of Life, which is the word of God, you must also drink. Thus, have something to drink to wash that Word down into your spirit, for it is written, "man shall not live by bread alone, but by every word that proceeds out of God's mouth" (Mat. 4:4).

FLOWING IN OVERFLOW

No one can know the intimate love of Christ until you drink this wine. Just do not drink to get filled; drink to be overflowing in the Spirit. To operate at the level that Jesus did, you must be overflowing, for He said greater works than these he will do (see John 14:12). The "he" referenced is the Believer or Child of God. Imagine this, greater than Him! WOW! This is awesome, for we serve an Awesome God.

Imagine this, He has called you to raise the dead, create new body parts, have the blind eyes healed, the deaf ears opened up, the mute speak, the lame or paralyzed to walk, and much, much, much, much more for those who believe and **"DO"** in Jesus' name. Again, the condition of this promise in John 14:12 is to believe in Jesus not just as Lord and

Savior but also as Healer, the Messiah or Anointed One that anoints to pour out on you the Holy Spirit of Fire (see Mat. 3:11).

Now the reason for greater works is not only to demonstrate the power of Jesus but also to demonstrate the power of His Father who sent Him. Jesus is revealed to us that show that God is our Father too. Jesus said, "the Father is greater than I" (John 14:28). Jesus does the same works but only because He has seen what the Father does (see John 5:19). As children of God, we are also expected to show that same power given by the Holy Spirit. So, drink the best wine.

Thus, by drinking the best wine, you receive or have an impartation of every Word that proceeds from the mouth of God which is Bible. You cannot have a prophetic word from the Holy Spirit without accurate discernment until you know His word.

It takes faith to understand the word of God. "Faith comes by hearing, and hearing by the word of God" (Rom. 10:17). "Now faith is assurance of things hoped for, proof of things not seen" (Heb. 11:1). The faith that our forefathers went out on is the same faith we are to have in this day and through the end of this age.

Just because you may not see all the results at one specific time does not mean it will not happen. If you hear God telling you something strange or to go beyond the realm of this world, have faith and do it. Everyone gets scared, and it is okay. Just believe the word that you are an Overcomer. It is by faith that what He is telling you is correct if it aligns with the Word of God or it is false. As long as you are actively moving and walking with Him, and if a mistake happens along the way, He will cover the blemish up with His mercy and grace.

Because "He who searches the hearts knows what is on the Spirit's mind, because he makes intercession for the saints according to God. We know that all things work together for good for those who love God, for those who are called according to his purpose" (Rom. 8:27-28).

HOW TO FLOW IN OVERFLOW

Now to drink the best wine: start by praying, which is to have an intimate conversation with the Father through the Holy Spirit that indwells you by seeking God with all your mind, body, and soul. Greet Him, then listen for a reply in which you will hear or discern Him through your inner man. The Holy Spirit speaks directly to your heart first, then your mind. Another way to drink the best wine is to listen to worship music that takes you into the throne room.

Be obedient to the call He commissions you to do. "For the gifts and the calling of God are irrevocable" (Rom. 11:29). If you are called to be in market-place ministry, which is in the business world by bringing the wealth of the nations to the body of Christ, so be it.

All ministries are for the building up of God's kingdom. The only thing that needs to come from the believer is Jesus' love for humanity. Just remember Jesus said, "these signs will accompany those who believe; in my name they will cast out demons; they will speak with new languages; they will take up serpents; and if they drink any deadly thing, it will in no way hurt them; they will lay hands on the sick, and they will recover" (Mark 16:17-18). The same condition of John 14:12 applies here; just believe, and the promise of this Scripture will accompany you.

God the Father and Jesus the Messiah have been directing the Holy Spirit to prepare the way for the new wineskins so that His best wine will be sent forth. The new wineskins are to be used with Holy Spirit fire as purifiers to reproduce more than what is comprehensible "new wineskins" with the harvest "new wine." I want to declare that this is true **firewater**. Not man-made wine but the actual wine that cleanses your spirit, soul, and body.

It is not about what any generation looks like but about your attitude and love for Jesus. God has everyone looking different to reach ALL tribes, tongues, and nations (see Rev. 5:9), social classes, whether conservative or non-conservative, we have to do whatever it takes to get the job done.

The heart that seeks after His face, not just His hands, will be fully used for the harvest army. God's children will take the kingdom of heaven by force (see Mat. 11:12). They are the warriors for today. It does not matter your age, as long as you believe in Jesus as Lord and Savior, you have been inducted into the army of the Lord.

This army is real because of the sense of urgency. They understand the need for training by spiritual mentors and seasoned veterans of Christ in the Holy Spirit spiritual war that has compassion for the lost, poor, and nation of Israel for it will be physically restored to its promised Abrahamic covenant territory (see Isa. 58:6-7; Rom. 10:26-27; Gen. 15:18-20), for the fulfillment of "the earth will be filled with the knowledge of Yahweh's glory, as the waters cover the sea" (Hab. 2:14).

How is this done? By being a Generation Zion warrior priest in the order of Melchizedek. The proclamation of preparation is done through Spiritual Warfare that is birthed in prayer. As this revival or others have termed The Third Great Awakening.

It must be understood that the proclamations that are made will always be Spiritual first then manifest physically according to our Father's will, not our will. For those that wait upon the Lord will be launched according to the plans that have been destined since before time began. Now, let us start proclaiming!

Chapter 2: THE GENERATION ZION PREPARATION

Proclaim this among the nations: "Prepare for war! Wake up the mighty men, let all the men of war draw near, let them come up. Beat your plowshares into swords and your pruning hooks into spears; Let the weak say, 'I am Strong.' Assemble and come, all you nations, and gather together all around. Cause Your mighty ones to go down there, O Lord" (Joel 3:9-11 NKJV).

PREPARE FOR WAR

God the Father, Son, and Holy Spirit have spoken the above message for thousands of years. But the truth standing behind that message has been taken lightly. The proclamation of Joel 3:9-11 has a two-fold meaning. It has been taught either as literal or allegorical, which is spiritualizing the literal. It needs to be taken both ways.

In the traditional view, God the Father will call the world to be prepared for the judgment of the Nations at the battle of Armageddon, which is at the end of the age when Jesus is beginning His physical 1,000-year reign as the King of kings on the Earth just not in the Spirit. It deals with the restoration of the entire boundaries of Israel, with Jerusalem being the capital of the world. All the believers on Earth who have accepted Jesus as Savior and Lord during the great tribulation will also be called into this battle.

The non-traditional view is that God the Father and Jesus the Messiah, through this powerful wave of the Holy Spirit, have started to fulfill the Joel 3:9-11 prophetic Scripture beginning on February 22, 2003, when Dr. C. Peter Wagner called for the new apostles and prophets to come forth of Generation "Z" or Generation "Zion." With this in mind, Father God is commanding the world and the Church to prepare for the great war of His wrath to come. Prepare yourselves for what is ahead.

HOW DOES IT APPLY TO THE CHURCH IN THIS HOUR?

War is always made on a spiritual level first before being manifested or revealed in the physical world (see Eph. 6:12). God is restoring the Church to a valuable state of Kingdom life, bringing a new breed of warriors, termed *warrior priests*. They will be obedient to His leadership. The Father and Jesus tells the Holy Spirit to condition the warriors to be sent out and used. The Church has gone through multiple generations of spiritual warfare for many centuries, mainly against itself. Bickering and quarreling against unnecessary doctrines split the body instead of bringing unity.

Since the restoration of the baptism of the Holy Spirit with the evidence of speaking in tongues of fire at Topeka, Kansas, and then Azusa St., Los Angeles, California, in 1906, the Church has been going through more intense battles with some of them still on an uphill slope with no view of reaching the pinnacle or top of the hill in order for the Church to go downhill and become entirely submitted to King Jesus, the ultimate Warrior High Priest.

In these last days, the battles are growing more intense, and God is bringing His beloved army into a higher level of spiritual warfare. The reason for this amount of intensity is only to remind Satan that Jesus has wiped "out the handwriting in ordinances which was against us. He has taken it out of the way, nailing it to the cross. Having stripped the principalities and the powers, he made a show of them openly, triumphing over them in it" (Col. 2:14-15). With that thought of knowledge, the devil knows that his time on Earth is growing shorter every moment that passes in these perilous days, and he wants to take anybody and everybody with him to hell and everlasting torment.

God is manifesting not just a theological illumination of the Church as a Bride waiting for the Bridegroom-King, but a refreshing illumination with a fresh revelation of the Bride, ready to receive the true

Bridegroom-King and Judge (see Isa. 61-63) to repopulate the Earth with warriors/warrior priests that seek after His actual presence. We will be stirred up with the fiery knowledge of the presence of the Father and the intimacy of the Son through the Holy Spirit with the knowledge and understanding of how to use His armor in practicality, not just theoretically. Christ is preparing the Church for His glorious appearance and return.

The beating of the plowshares and pruning hooks of Joel 3:10 are symbolic of weapons of peace in the time of war that is at hand. The swords and the spears are the weapons of war. God says, "to turn the weapons of peace into weapons of war, which is the Holy Scriptures and the Rhema WORD to Life." If you are reading this, you are a warrior/priest, and I implore you to use the Living Word of God planted in your heart that eases your soul to be used carefully as fuel against Satan and his minions, not your fellow Christian. The weapon being described is the Sword of the Spirit (the written and spoken Word of God).

WARRIORS THAT ARE FARMERS

Paul reminds Timothy in 2 Timothy 2:3-13 that he is a warrior as well as a farmer. Timothy was a part of the early church community, and leaders in that era as seen as examples for the Church in this current time. Timothy was a warrior first, then a farmer. That is why we should first be warriors, then farmers.

The Sowers in Jesus' times would be equivalent to today's farmers because they (like every believer in Christ) must labor for what they sow in the field (see Mat. 13). As farmers or Sowers, we the Church must endure seasons of weather changes to receive a great harvest. A Sower must have patience, endurance, and perseverance. The only way patience, endurance, and perseverance will be brought about is by having faith in God, knowing that His agape or Greek translation "unconditional" love toward what we have planted will produce not just a seed but a tree in the middle of a beautiful garden.

Remember that there are also different seasons of weather, not just spring and summer but also autumn and winter. All those seasons are essential and needed in life to properly cultivate the harvest that represents God's different people in our daily path to help them grow and mature. I define those meetings as Divine appointments. While we reap the harvest, at the same time, we should be sowing seeds in the ground to continue reaping a harvest.

When the difficult seasons of life occur, endure them as Christ endured the sufferings of the cross. It was not easy for Him to endure that pain and suffering, but He endured it because of His sacrificial love for all humanity. If He can endure that pain and punishment for us, we can endure all the trials and tribulations that come toward us to build character and reliance on the Holy Spirit.

The storms of life cause disastrous effects on people by either attacking them spiritually or emotionally, which can be mentally or physically with a combination of any of the above mentioned. If we, the Bride, have our eyes on the Bridegroom Jesus, He will put us in the eye of the storms of life that are also referred to in the Bible as trials and tribulations (see John 16:33; Jam. 1:2 NKJV). The "eye" is the center of any storm and is the calmest point within it. When you are in the middle of it, none of it can or should affect you. All you should know is "Christ's love which surpasses knowledge, that you may be filled with all the fullness of God" (Eph. 3:19). It with Christ's love that there is victory in your life.

The victory comes not just from overcoming that particular storm but by trusting in the One who overcame all storms, Jesus Christ. It is where you are constantly being filled with all the fullness of God, this is the fulfillment of moving from "glory to glory" (2 Cor. 3:18) for "we are more than conquerors through him who loved us" (Rom. 8:37) "but we also rejoice in our sufferings, knowing that suffering produces perseverance; and perseverance, proven character; and proven character, hope" (Rom. 5:3-4) and that hope is eternal life through Jesus Christ our Savior (see Tit. 3:7).

When we have shown the victory of Jesus, by standing on the Solid Rock, who is Jesus, and going through that tribulation or test we become more like Him revealing the glory of the Father through the Holy Spirit by being faithful for what He promises that "He is able to do exceedingly abundantly above all that we ask or think" (Eph. 3:20 NKJV). Before you go on, reread this paragraph and reflect on the passage of "able to do exceedingly abundantly," knowing that God is more than capable to supply not just your daily needs but able **to go beyond anything** you need.

Remember this true saying "the bigger the trial or test, the bigger the reward is." If God cannot trust you with the little things in life that cause growing pains, and they do hurt, how can He trust you with the bigger things? Little is much when God is in it. So, stick with the trial, go on through the pain, whatever it is and get through it by constantly communicating with Father God. Stay grounded in His Word and promises that Abba Father gives you. Because God through the Holy Spirit "himself is who goes before you. He will be with you. He will not fail you nor forsake you" (Deut. 31:8) and "count it all joy, my brothers, when you fall into various temptations, knowing that the testing of your faith produces endurance. Let endurance have its perfect work, that you may be perfect and complete, lacking in nothing" (Jas. 1:2-4). Have an elder accountability partner of the same gender; stay rooted in a local church that God selects for you. Stand behind that local pastor, for he is your watchman set to guide you through life's struggles and victories. Before God, he must answer for every sheep given to Him at the judgment seat of Christ. So, love him, and he will love you more for loving him. Treat him with the same respect you request, which will honor God because it is written, "obey your leaders and submit to them, for they watch on behalf of your souls, as those who will give account, that they may do this with joy, and not with groaning, for that would be unprofitable for you" (Heb. 13:17).

As warrior farmers, our first job is to defend the crops from illegal fires, plagues, floods, weeds, and tares, which the enemy is allowed to plant during various times in our life to keep us on our guard. The harvest will not be ripe without the proper tools or weapons "we don't wage war according to the flesh" (2 Cor. 10:3). The proper tools are the armor of God, the priesthood garments, and the gifts of the Spirit that our lives depend upon. We reap what we sow (see Gal. 6:7).

We must have confidence in Christ that none of the harvest shall fall on the wayside. If we have on the whole armor of God, all we should be "able to do is stand against the schemings of the devil" (Eph. 6:11 NKJV). The key is to stand and be firm because God's armor will do it all by staying clothed in Him. Even "if we are faithless, He remains faithful; He cannot deny Himself" (2 Tim. 2:13 NKJV). That is the assurance that even without any faith in our lives and if we feel like it is time to give up, Jesus will not give up on us, for we are a part of Him.

Even if the individual sower is laboring in a certain way that he does not think he will have a successful seed planted, the Holy Spirit will always allow that seed to be planted by that sower. The soil, which is the human heart, may be hard, but the living water, who is the Holy Spirit, will soften the ground, for He alone pricks or cuts the unbeliever's hearts (see Acts 2:37).

The "weak people" referenced in Joel 3:10 are humble in heart. They apply that "whatever you (the believer in Christ Jesus/Generation Zion) do in word or deed, do all in the name of the Lord Jesus, giving thanks to God the Father through Him" (Col. 3:17 NKJV). For our strength comes from the Lord to be clothed in humility. When the weak say, "I am strong," it shows need and dependence on God, their maker. Dependence is a vital issue. For without Him, we can do nothing. Remember, "I can do all things through Christ, who strengthens me" (Phil. 4:13), for the Anointed One has given us His strength to go out and do all that He has called us to do.

Joel 3:11 speaks of assembling all the nations, which our Heavenly Father declared in Revelation 5:9 that every tribe, tongue, and nation will be called to Him to be inducted into the army of the Lord Jesus that He is sending out. The establishment of this army is what the Lord has been preparing and building since the day of Pentecost, the birth of the Church. Every generation has had its leaders and armies.

As one of the Generation Zion leaders serving the greatest Commander and Chief, it is time for the Church to prepare for His mighty ones to go down there, O Lord (see Joel 3:11). With Generation Zion they are the beginning of gathering the "mighty ones" for this great battle of Armageddon at the end of this age. The elect of all the past ages, whether in heaven or on the Earth with the warring angels, will be included with Generation "ZION." So, let us go and prepare for war!

HARVEST TIME

Generation Zion is the last or terminal generation that has a chance to reach the world before the coming of the Lord Jesus Christ. We must prepare for the Lord of the Harvest, Jesus Christ, for the outpouring. Jesus said, "the harvest indeed is plentiful, but the laborers are few. Pray therefore that the Lord of the harvest will send out laborers into his harvest" (Mat. 9:37-38).

All I can say is, "The Harvest is HERE! The HARVEST IS HERE!!" The whole world is the harvest, but who will go out? We need Sowers and laborers. Generation Zion will be the last laborers of the harvest. But God has saved the best for last with a greater anointing than previously seen.

The Bible speaks about a great apostasy coming in the last days (see 2 The. 2:3). I believe and know from personal experience that it is true since it is here now. It has been manifesting its ugly head slowly but surely over the past fifty or so years.

That apostasy is the love of the Church growing cold right before the world's eyes. There are moments when the love of those who serve in the world is better than the love of the so-called "servants" in the Church, but not much. But with such an apostasy or falling away from the first love comes a greater harvest built on unconditional love. Those who do not think they want Jesus will scream out His name. In the darkest of all places, the seed planted through *this* generation will give God and His Son Jesus the Messiah all power, honor, and glory. God knows each individual by name, anointing, rank, and loves them unconditionally. They have died to themselves, obedient to the Holy Spirit, and love their lives not unto death.

The harvest will be filled with power and presence evangelism accompanied by signs, wonders, healings, and miracles worthy to the Giver of gifts. Great revivalists such as Charles G. Finney, John G. Lake, Smith Wigglesworth, Maria Woodworth-Etter, Aimee Semple McPherson, Kathryn Kuhlman, Oral Roberts, etc. carried that power and evangelism to the very core of their being.

Modern-day presence evangelism is known by Tommy Tenney, International House of Prayer, the Brownsville revival, Toronto Airport, The Call, etc. "Presence evangelism" is the call of the prophets and seers. Modern day prophets are Bill Hamon, Rick Joyner, James Goll to name a few. How is this carried out?

It is carried out because of their fiery dedication to the love of Jesus and the truth for which He calls us to walk in. That same fiery dedication must still be caught in modern evangelism, revivals, prophetic flow of the Holy Spirit to win the world to Christ and bring conviction. Generation Zion will walk in an anointing greater than Jesus, who ministered with the Spirit without measure (see John 3:34). No limitations in the Spirit realm.

When God uses people that are completely sold out to Him, His glory cannot in any other way do anything but be caught. This is what the harvest laborers will be doing during this time. Taking the tools (gifts) that God the Father instructs the Holy Spirit to distribute to us for the process of digging, sowing, which is also planting and plowing one seed at a time until the last seed is finished maturing. Jesus said, "this Good News of the Kingdom will be preached in the whole world for a testimony to all the nations, and then the end will come" (Mat. 24:14). Well, the end is near because the Gospel or Good News of the Kingdom is spreading to all the nations. This is it. This is the time to prepare and send the laborers so that Jesus can come.

WHAT HAPPENED TO THE PREVIOUS HARVEST LABORERS IN THE USA?

There has been a continual revival process on this continent for over 500 years. The foundations of the United States of America are based on the principles of God. Many have passed away not seeing the fruit of the harvest grow but just planting seeds for the generations after them. Because of their prayers, the Lord is faithful in answering those prayers because they are His incense before His throne day and night (see Rev. 5:8).

For God is faithful and does not forget those that died here in America and practiced the ways of the Kingdom to ALL nations on this continent. He remembers those saints and has honored them for their obedience to the true gospel of Christ. Because of the different nationalities, there has been racial segregation among all nations in America. People tend to forget they are gentiles in the flesh. A gentile is a gentile as a Jew is a Jew, and the respect for one another and treating each other like brothers and sisters has not been passed down through the years. The **Church of America has forgotten its roots** and those that have stayed true and faithful to God through Jesus Christ.

The Church of America primarily has been influenced by worldly viewpoints instead of the Church shaping the world. It has become either spiritually impotent or spiritually deformed. Having no ability to conceive and reproduce itself or is birthing children with deformities that are instilled with hypocrisy, judgment, gossip which is slander, false agendas, and motives, all forms of immorality plus a non-centered gospel that has removed many of the primary and core teachings of the Lord Jesus Christ as being non-effective for the dispensation or stewardship of Grace.

Through all those spiritual birth defects, does the motto "In God We Trust" engraved on the United States of America's one-dollar bill have any real meaning to it? If it does, it is only to the true believers of Jesus Christ. Many will say they believe in Jesus but do not confess to the practice of His teachings.

Jesus said, "If you love Me, keep My commandments" (John 14:15 NKJV). He only spoke two commandments or rules of living in the Gospels, and they are a summary of the Law of Moses. Many choose not to keep His commands, and they are to "you shall love the Lord your God with all your heart, and with all your soul, and with all your mind, and with all your strength.' This is the first commandment. The second is like this, 'You shall love your neighbor as yourself.' There is no other commandment greater than these" (Mark 12:30-31).

The first commandment that Jesus spoke of is a summary of the first four commandments of Moses's law written upon the first tablet, which describes the relationship between man to God the Father. The second commandment spoken is the condensing of the last six commandments of the Law of Moses written on the second tablet, which describes how humans should treat one another. They are the most straightforward commandments to follow, yet the Church has many problems following them.

Thus, the motto "In God We Trust" has been a great laugh for our adversary, the devil. Does America really trust in God? Only at the verge of destruction only a few do but, in reality, America does not. But I want you to think and search your inner man about this question "Does God really trust in America?" I believe He does, or He would have annihilated it. I must emphasize that Satan has taken away the privileges of the Church in America little by little. The God that

America should trust is **not** the god it is trusting in. Satan has masqueraded himself as trying to be God (see Isa. 14:14).

When it came to taking a stand for what was right, what did the Church of America do? The Church DID ABSOLUTELY NOTHING! We had the right to defend our beliefs, but through the twisting of the Constitution's First Amendment with the Separation of Church and State, we lost the right to stand up for ourselves. All the Church had to do was pray and not sit back idly. That was the beginning of lawlessness in the Church of America.

Paul said, "don't be weary in doing what is right" (2 The. 3:13). The good and doing what is right that Paul writes about has to do is with defending the principles of the Word of God. For a Biblical example of not growing weary of doing good, read the book of Esther. It is a biography of how God used the willingness of this simple Jewish girl to save her people by taking a stand for her people by upholding God's truth and justice through prayer and fasting.

Jesus said, "because iniquity will be multiplied, the love of many will grow cold.But he who endures to the end will be saved" (Mat. 24:12-13). The Greek rendered in this passage to "grow cold" means to "blow with a mighty wind hard like wax." Can you believe that those believers that have grown cold continue to grow colder and colder? At one time in their life, they were filled with the love and fire of Christ, and now it has grown dim. It also demonstrates that for those that keep the love or continually renew it and endure the stressful times, their fire of love that wants to dim shall be saved. I am not saying they are not Christians because salvation is by faith in Jesus Christ through the grace of God the Father, and that is the only way to salvation.

The Church of America has grown cold. How did that happen? Because of iniquity and lawlessness in the land, the Church has not functioned as a corporate body. The elders in the Church did not take a stand for biblical principles. They appear to have a false sense of religion and have conformed to the world's ways. Thus, God has allowed their hearts to "grow cold like wax."

They are portrayed to have a form of godliness but deny the power (see 2 Tim. 3:5) of Jesus which has left them spiritually cold and some dead. They were once light carriers. Now they are dead carriers allowing themselves to be used by the enemy as a wind of darkness to try and blow out the fire of the Lord among the Spirit-filled body. It cannot be done because you cannot fight God and win. Remember, "if God is for us who can be against us?" (Rom. 8:31).

WHAT WAS LOST IN THE USA?

We lost, particularly in the secular schools of America, the right to pray in class. The Ten Commandments were taken out of the school, and "all hell has broken out since." Nietzsche proclaimed that "God is dead," and the Church has allowed that philosophy and thought to penetrate the minds of the American public with horrible ramifications in just a few generations. I want to say that my God is not dead but alive forevermore!

The Church gave the devil an inch, and like always, he takes a mile. That inch was one too many. He may be the "prince of the power of the air" (Eph. 2:2) and the "ruler of this world" (John 12:31). Still, Jesus is the King of the universe, which is continually growing and expanding in all directions because it can never contain the full Shekinah glory of the Father "for the Earth is the Lord's and all its fullness" (Psa. 24:1; 1 Cor. 10:28).

Now there has been an increase in violence in schools. The teachings of creation were thrown out as mere fairy tales. Evolution became "normal thinking." Lustful passions became part of the "normal culture." The culture of America reflects the New Testament city of Corinth.

John Hagee wrote the following in his *Prophecy Study Bible*:

> Corinth, the most important city in Greece during Paul's day, was a bustling hub of worldwide commerce, degraded

culture and idolatrous religion...This cosmopolitan center thrived on commerce, entertainment, vice, and corruption; pleasure-seekers came there to spend money on a holiday from morality. Corinth became so notorious for its evils that the term *Korinthiazomai* ("to act like a Corinthian") became a synonym for debauchery and prostitution.[1]

Debauchery is given in two meanings in *Webster's Revised Unabridged Dictionary*:

1. Corruption of fidelity; seduction from virtue, duty, or allegiance.
2. Excessive indulgence of the appetites; especially, excessive indulgence of lust; intemperance; sensuality; habitual lewdness.[2]

The combination of the above meanings for debauchery accurately describes the Nation of America. The corruption in America stems from us not taking a stand for what we should believe in. What is wrong is right and what is right is wrong. The Church of America does not stand up for what it truly believes in, and those that do are very few in this day and age. They are afraid of any form of persecution. To be persecuted is honorable because if the world did not like Christ and persecuted Him, why should they like us and not persecute us? (see John 15:20). It is time to stand up and be firm in our beliefs, Oh Church of America!

Like all cultures not conformed to the image of God through Christ, it will become wicked. Two wicked cities in the Old Testament are Sodom and Gomorrah. If no repentance happens in a city, God will destroy cities like Sodom, Gomorrah, and Corinth. God used angels in the spirit realm to destroy the cities, but the destruction appeared to be from natural disasters. Before its rebuilding in 1858 as AcroCorinth, the city of Corinth was destroyed by an Earthquake in 521 A.D. I can imagine the angels' feet stamping or, in another aspect, dancing to the beat of worship and praise of the Almighty with the results of the city being flattened out with the physical appearance of an Earthquake.

If America does not truly repent for all its demonic, self-centered, and prideful actions, there will be consequences greater than that of Genesis 19 and the city of Corinth. God sent two angels to warn Lot's family about the coming destruction of Sodom and Gomorrah because Abraham interceded for him and his family to God (see Gen. 18:16-33).

Genesis 19:13, 24-25 says:

> "For we (the two angels) will destroy this place, because the outcry against them has grown so great before Yahweh that Yahweh has sent us to destroy it"...Then Yahweh rained on Sodom and on Gomorrah sulfur and fire from Yahweh out of the sky. He overthrew those cities, all the plain, all the inhabitants of the cities, and that which grew on the ground.

The Church should be interceding for one another and has lost sight of that. It should also be caring and witnessing to the lost, the sick, the elderly, the widows, and the orphans. Those commissions have not been correctly functioning either. If you desire to see a particular city inhabited by Christ, start praying and fasting for that city, especially for unsaved friends who are part of that community. If not, destruction and ruin will come about.

The stench of sin in this country has gone up to the face of the Lord, and He is tired of it. He gave us a small demonstration of the Day of the Lord spoken of in Joel, Ezekiel, Thessalonians, Peter, Jude, Revelation, and other passages of the Bible. God used the consequential destruction of the Twin Towers in New York City on September 11, 2001, to turn the hearts of the Americans back to Him, but it only happened for a short amount of time.

At that time, America had increased the numbers of people coming to Church. But how many churches can say that they kept the harvest going? Not a lot. Some did. But the majority did not. Why? Because they never kept the fire lit, for there was not enough oil in the lamps (see Mat. 25:1:1-13). Because the Church is full of religion and hypocrisy, and judgment. Many of those who came in for that harvest feast left "burnt out."

- Religion defined in this book is applied to the Christian who has a mindset of Biblical values and standards that contradict the two commandments of Christ. They act like the Pharisees in the New Testament, that have a controlling and dominant personality. They tend to mask and work in conjunction with a combination of two spirits known as Jezebel and Delilah. They tend to act like heathen (ungodly) Gentiles in their administration of discipline in the Church, not showing compassion.
- Hypocrisy is defined as the actions of a hypocrite.
- A hypocrite is a person falsely portraying a holy person. That is when the individual pretends to be full of the Spirit of God when in reality, they are full of themselves, the devil, or both. They contradict God's word, judge people by their standards, and are proud of how they live.

Jesus says four things about hypocrites. They are:

Legalistic (Mat. 5:20)[3]

Hypocrites say they know the Word of God but have no reflection of the Author and Finisher of the Word of God. They have *only* head knowledge and *no* heart knowledge. God desires to have the willing vessel or person be filled *with* head *and* heart knowledge.

Prideful (see Mat. 23:5-7)[4]

Hypocrites think that they are "the all-powerful ones" and that everyone must cater to, bow to, or worship them. They want to sit in the best places because of their education or name. There is only one who deserves any of this. His name is Jesus Christ of Nazareth.

Harmful to others (see Mat. 23:13-15)[5]

Hypocrites add more laws to people's lives, for example, "Jesus plus this or Jesus plus that." I say it is "Jesus plus nothing, Jesus only." They teach tradition that is not part of the Word or twists the Word to fit what they believe is God's truth. They bind the person with rules instead of freeing them with love. They also want self-glory, which will be their reward.

Opposing to the character and purpose of God (see Mat. 23:29-33)[6]

Hypocrites like to play God. They take His place for judging and judgment. They take vengeance when God says, "Vengeance is Mine, I will repay," says the Lord. And again, "The Lord will judge His people" (Heb. 10:30). When God judges, it is with justice. When hypocrites judge, it is with condemnation. The purpose of God through Jesus is to save sinners, clean them up, love them and free them from all oppression and depression from the world, the devil, and the hypocritical churches that choose to bash and smash instead of love.

Jesus loves the sinners and is their best friend and advocate. He loves people and hates sin. The Church has taken its right to judge and gone beyond its limits. The Church of America has gone from fervent love for righteousness to fervent condemnation. What we lost most of all was the respect of the Father because of how the Church handled the harvest of 9/11. It was not taken as seriously as it should have been. Much wheat was lost due to a genuine lack of the Father's unconditional love for mankind.

He still loves us, the Church, and He will not quit loving us because He sees the blood of Jesus on us. "God is love" (1 John 4:16 NKJV). But He is disappointed that He gave the Church of America a great opportunity to minister to the lost and dying of this land during that harvest, and some of the leaders of that harvest did not fully take advantage of it. The harvest time of 9/11 is over with. Now it is time to stand up and train Generation Zion for the GREAT HARVEST. This is the harvest of "agapao' or unconditional love in action. This is the Greek word that rendered "love" according to John 3:16.

THE THREE R'S: RENEWAL – REVOLUTION – REVIVAL

The Great Harvest has been given to Generation Zion to fulfill. God ordained us to live in times such as these to spread the Gospel of the Kingdom using a broken youth that is set on fire (Jacob), a parental generation that will mentor Generation Zion with all that they know (Isaac), and a grandparent generation that will be able to walk in a wisdom that supersedes the Isaacs with unquestioning wisdom from the Holy Spirit (Abraham), that will have no problems loving the great Savior, Jesus Christ. There are three ordained parts for the Great Harvest to flourish. In addition to these three generations comes a generation of praise or a generation of Judah.

The renewal leaders will be the grandparents and parents of the Generation Zion revolutionaries. The process between revolution and revival will be a quick one. The Pentecostal and Charismatic leaders should be considered the parents of the Renewal leaders and are the grandparents or Abrahams of Generation "ZION." The Renewal leaders are the Isaacs, and the pure Revivalists of Generation Zion are the Jacobs.

This threefold harvest generation is broken down by renewal, revolution, and revival. The Great Harvest will peak during the Generation Zion revival.

RENEWAL

There must be an accurate and adequate definition of terms for renewal, revolution, and revival that needs to be fulfilled during the Great Harvest. The most detailed description to date for "renewal" is described by Ché Ahn in his book *Into the Fire*:

> "Renewal" is the sovereign refreshing God is bringing to His Church and those already a part of it. It is glorious, needed, and welcomed. As John Arnott declares, "This move of the Spirit is first of all about a renewal and refreshing for Christians, finding out what a wonderful, loving Savior we have; second, it is about loving our neighbor-evangelism."[7]

The reason for renewal first is to have a significantly restored relationship with the Father through the blood of Jesus the Son, by sending the Holy Spirit who indwells and empowers us to experience a variety of times of refreshment and healings within our mind, spirit, soul, and body. With this renewal comes a grave responsibility of cherishing the anointing, power, and relationship that the Father has established within the Church while continuing to shower the Church with blessings. The relationship restored is on the purest joy not known by human terms except that the result of it will be by our relationship and obedience to Him. It is from a loving Heavenly Father to a child that has received a command that he (the child) knows he is honorable to his Father.

The renewal was birthed from a set of passionate believers who longed for the tangible presence of God, that sparked a renewed wave of glory that has not been seen since the early days of the Church. This only came about from praying and fasting for a great revival. This type of passion can only be given to God the Father, who sent Jesus, "the Lamb of God who takes away the sin of the world!" (John 1:29). John the Baptist had it, and so did those believers.

The definition for this type of "passion" to/for God is "being totally, completely, all the way sold out to the One that we are made in the image and likeness of and that '**we love what He loves, and we hate what He hates**' burns within every fiber, cell, and nucleus of our being." Just remember we are called to hate the sin in the world that contaminates the person and not the person.

We still have a sinful nature which is referred to in Paul's letters as the "old man" (Eph. 4:22). Even though "it," the old man, is crucified with Christ and dead. This does not mean that, at times, it likes to resuscitate during the oddest times to bring condemnation to people forgetting that it itself was once condemned.

Since 1994, several churches in the United States of America have experienced this renewal. It has brought nothing but many blessings to the congregation. The visitors for the renewal will continue to touch many more unseen people in the body until "revolution" comes out in full glory. Renewal prepares for the "revolution" of the Great Harvest, the next move of the Spirit that will be very mighty and instrumental for God's kingdom.

Reiterating the illustration from John 2 of the wineskin/new wine that this renewal process that the Church has been in is the beginning of the out-pouring of the best wine to come. All I want to say is that the cover is open. What has been going on spiritually is that God has only allowed the smell or aroma of the wine to be distributed throughout the world. The new wine has yet to impact the Church body as a whole.

The wine connoisseur/expert has the ability to tell how good the wine is just by smelling it. The older the wine is, the better the quality and taste. Until now the past generations have only had the ability to smell the wine, but Generation Zion will have the ability to smell and taste the new wine. The taste buds of Generation Zion are just getting ready to savor the best wine that has been kept before the foundations of the ages of the universe/world.

International House of Prayer - IHOP

A release from the Spirit birthed during this renewal process has been the International House of Prayer, IHOP, not to be confused with the International House of Pancakes. Its structure is based upon the fulfillment of Acts 15:14-18, which is the rebuilding of the tabernacle of David. The tabernacle of David was built on poles, but it was a place of ministry that an individual could attend and be ministered to by the Holy Spirit 24 hours a day, 7 days a week.

Kansas City, MO, is where the IHOP was birthed in the United States of America. Other IHOPs have been planted in major cities and have been successful, with many more on the way. These IHOPs have been produced as training grounds for Generation "ZION." The IHOP is a place of refuge for the individual to be prayed for, ministered to by the leadership teams that the Holy Spirit are led by. It is also a place of acceptance and knowing that God's genuine power and love are fulfilled there.

The musical concept of IHOP is to read a portion of Scripture and let the singers and instrumentalists have the leading of the Holy Spirit to "sing to Yahweh a new song! Sing to Yahweh, all the earth. Sing to Yahweh! Bless his name! Proclaim his salvation from day to day! Declare his glory among the nations, his marvelous works among all the peoples" (Psa. 96:1-3).

The mature Church has nothing to do with physical or spiritual age but a combination of both. Significant portions of the body are infantile and are sucking on their bottles of spiritual milk. They have not accepted the process, responsibility, and command to maturity by applying the meaty sections of the Word to their life. They are overgrown babies.

The Godhead has agreed that it is time for them to wake up and go through some trials and tribulations for dependence on Him and purge the "poor me and I only" mindsets. They have not accepted that "we have the mind of Christ" (1 Cor. 2:16 NKJV). There is no capital "I" or "ME" in "Him."

The immature believers need to come to maturity through the refiner's fire (see Zec. 13:9; Mal. 3:2) because they need to come out as fully refined workable vessels. This purging process is for all believers, immature and mature. The first reason for this is that the immature ones will not feel that they are alone in this process. The second reason for the refiner's fire upon the whole body is that the mature believers do not develop a sense of pride within themselves. This refining process is a daily one.

During the renewal process, God has been laying down many foundations for reconciliation of generations, racial and cultural reconciliation and redemption, unity between the body of Christ and the denial of the one-person show, and the strength of the five-fold Apostolic Church moving in all glory and power in the last apostolic age. These are necessary steps for the revolution.

Considering what God is doing in these last days, I am excited, honored, and privileged to have been able to participate in the latter half of the renewal process. The exciting aspect is that God is preparing to release the revolution of Generation Zion for the upcoming revival that billions of souls will believe and trust in Jesus as their Savior, King, Lord, Healer, and much, much, much more during the Great Harvest.

REVOLUTION

The second of the three part ministerial plan for the Great Harvest is "revolution."

The definition of revolution is "a sudden or momentous change in a situation".[8] Jesus proclaimed, "Do you think that I have come to give peace in the earth? I tell you, no, but rather division" (Luk. 12:51). Jesus's whole ministry was about division. That type of division spoken about is revolution. As a result of revolution, division happens. The revolution that causes division is right versus wrong, good versus evil, merited war versus unmerited peace, love versus condemnation, and liberty versus captivity. The warfare that has been proclaimed since that day is spiritual and not just a physical war that the Jews were seeking. The peace spoken in the Bible is of the mind, will, emotions, and not a worldly peace.

Revolution must not be confused with reformation. The reformation was about change. The reformation was good but did not complete the job needed for today. The reformation that God used with Martin Luther brought about the truth that salvation is by grace alone and not by good works. During that time, the Roman Catholic Church had for its time a monopoly of oppression on the people and taught works-based salvation that it never liberated the believers. The Reformation birthed modern Protestantism.

There is a cry among many intercessors, and those that feel God's heart wrenched desire for change within Christendom for revolution. The prayers have been recorded on tapes, CDs, MP3s, YouTube™, Spotify™, etc. Those prayers have been heard, and now the time has come for them to be answered. Our God in Heaven has been waiting to release this new glory on the Bride of Jesus. Because of religious natures in the Church, His hands have been tied.

No one sought for "this" sudden change until recently. Many have asked for change, but not enough. It only takes a spark to set a fire. The spark has been caught. No one will hinder God's will and desire for Generation "ZION." No man on Earth can stop what is happening.

This is a God thing and not a man thing. For the secret plans of God are being released to the body and are manifesting.

This revolution will turn the Church upside down first. The restoration of the mindset of the first century Church is manifesting in the twenty-first century Church. It is still Christ's body, just a different set of individuals. Same Spirit in operation, just a different season in God's plan.

The time of renewal is ending in a season of purging. The purpose is for consecration, and dedication, while getting back down to the basics and roots of God through Jesus Christ because we, the Church, have gotten off the original focus of renewal. We have turned it into a "bless me Lord" club. God is restoring His "agapao" or unconditional love in action and fear of Him into us (His body).

For this significant change to come about, purging must start in the House of God. Jesus said, "first remove the beam out of your own eye, and then you can see clearly to remove the speck out of your brother's eye" (Mat. 7:5). We, the mature Church, must remove our "planks" from our eyes that have been allowed to be shoved in by the enemy. The beams have been shoved in due to arrogance, shameful lusts, ritualistic and undeserved dogmatic views of the Word. The revolution will take the beams out of the body's spiritual eyes and allow His body to remove the specks from our brothers' (all of humanity's) eyes.

When you study the teachings of Jesus to the seven churches of Asia Minor in Revelations 2 and 3, you will find that they are models of every local church. Five of the seven churches were judged as having errors in them, and two of those churches were error-free. That shows that 5/7ths of the body is in error in some way or another. That leaves only 2/7ths clean.

The Church should strive to model after the two error-free churches. They were Smyrna and Philadelphia. The local bodies that are modeling either after Smyrna, Philadelphia, or a model of both will be able to help remove the planks from the rest of the body through the "agapao" love of Christ in the Spirit with no condemnation. I have to say, "He who has an ear, let him hear what the Spirit says to the assemblies" (Rev. 2:7, 11, 17, 29, 3:6, 13, 22).

New Church Government

It is during this season that a new Church government will be established, and the change is being brought about in this very hour of writing. The apostles and prophets have been put on the shelf and suppressed by the pastors and teachers. They (the apostles and prophets) that have been restored last shall be used first. Those called into pastoral ministry will still function and are needed, but not at the capacity they were allowed. The pastors of old secluded the body from one another and looked at it as their people, not God's people. That is how cliques start, and God is destroying that.

Each local body will sow into a more extensive body covered by an apostolic network. Every apostolic network must work together for the common goal of the upcoming harvest or revival or awakening. There will be diversity among the believers. Individuality mixed with unity will be the theme of the networks because "there are many members, but one body" (1 Cor. 12:20).

The makeup of the new council will be the restored fully functional Generation "ZION." This governmental lifestyle has not been known since the birthing of the Church, where the fear of the Lord and God's perpetual "agapao" love expressed simultaneously. These leaders will all flow in the apostolic wisdom combined with other gifts manifesting.

The new Church councils will all be apostolic and prophetic in nature but not always with those labels. They will be seeking God's face and direction as warrior priests. Majority of the churches during this day and age limit God's power. Generation Zion will not put God in a box and limit His unlimited power. They will equip the local body and send them out. No more pew sitting, just pew warming.

There will be a true sense of Spiritual timing among Generation "ZION." This Generation will include the following traits: true humility, integrity, and "agapao" love.

Among the three listed traits. I feel integrity should be discussed. Other authors have written about true humility and will not be discussed. More is written on "agapao" love in chapter 3.

INTEGRITY OF GENERATION ZION

The integrity and accountability will be very high but will have a lot of love and mercy. They will be able to forgive and walk in that forgiveness. They will be able to hand out forgiveness to others that need it to see them set free. For freedom and forgiveness goes hand in hand. Generation Zion "babes in Christ" (see 1 Cor. 3:1 KJV) will seek mentors that are full of the Spirit and not ruled by their flesh. Their flesh will be under control.

This type of integrity is needed for the harvest, each laborer must be accountable to one another. The Church has had many scandals over the past fifty to sixty years because of either "lust of the flesh, the lust of the eyes, and the pride of life" (1 John 2:16). When those individuals were in trouble, they called on God but did not call on their accountability partner. God always provides a way out of sin. He is tired of having His people mocked by the world because of their unwillingness to submit to Him.

REVIVAL

The last part of this threefold ministerial plan for the great harvest is revival or Great Awakening. Revival is accurately described in Ché Ahn's book *Into the Fire*:

> Revival, then, is the *continuum* of this wave as it sweeps over the community at large. When it hits, a great awakening occurs, and an unusually large number of non-Christians are brought into the Kingdom in a relatively short time period. Everything changes. God becomes a central focus of the

community. This then is what I am longing for. Revival with a capital *R*. A historic revival where a whole nation is changed.[9]

When Ché is describing revival and says it is "the continuum of this wave," the wave he is referring to is renewal. But I would encourage that the continuing wave is also built on the upcoming renewal revolution. From revolution, then is revival. I am also in complete agreement with Ché about the historic revival to come that it will be so big and grand that it will not have the ability to be contained in just one section of a city or town. How great is our God!

Revival will be all over the city or town like a blazing fire of glory. You will hear about the outpouring of God in one place and another place, and then another place. You will not know who is doing what because the Holy Spirit will be ministering His "apagao" love towards God's children that are ready to be welcomed into the Father's kingdom.

Be aware that with this type of love comes a cloud by day and fire by night. A sense of Holy fear will come upon many people and cry out, "OH GOD, I AM NOT WORTHY! FOR YOU ARE SO HOLY!" Are you ready for this? Are you? Just pray and do what the Holy Spirit instructs you to do. Don't rebel. Just submit.

Chapter 3: THE GENERATION ZION AGAPAO! (UNCONDITIONAL LOVE IN ACTION)

The Generation Zion army of warrior priests will be the refined vessels of "agapao" love. Why? Because they "love [agapao] Him [God], because He first loved [agapao] us" (1 John 4:19). They also follow "this commandment we have from him [Jesus Christ]: that he who loves [agapao] God should also love [agapao] his brother" (1 John 4:21).

WHAT IS LOVE?

Love can be defined in many ways. But the true meaning is defined in the New Testament as *agape* pronounce "ah gah pay." In 1 John 4:8 it is written that "God is love," or God is "agape." It, therefore, is part of God's nature or also defined as an attribute. The love of God and Christ is unconditional (see John 15:9). Abide in it. Live in it.

Agape is the first fruit of the Spirit according to Galatians 5:22. According to the Greek language, all the fruit is given in feminine forms. As the Bride of Christ and our relationship to Jesus Christ our Bridegroom. I bring this up because we are defined by the original meaning of masculine and feminine. As the Bride, thinking of the relationship that Jesus will marry us at the Great Wedding Supper of the Lamb, He wants our love to be pure towards one another (see John 15:17).

It is to be used to build relations and nurture one another. Relationship-building is defined as "teaching, for reproof, for correction, and for instruction in righteousness, that each person who belongs to God may be complete, thoroughly equipped for every good work" (2 Tim. 3:16-17). I also want to say that agape is defined according to 1 Cor. 13:4-7 where "Agape is..." an unconditional love that goes beyond a range of limits and persists regardless of circumstance, emotions, thoughts, or attitude. It goes to the extent of seeking the best for others. Counts others as better than oneself (see Phil. 2:3), for this is the will of the Father. Remember, we are sent to provide Abba's love to His creation through agape.

LOVE IN ACTION

When Christ talks about his relationship between the Love of God and the Love of Christ, its usage is used as a verb in Greek. "ah gah pah oh." Another way to view it is "Love in action." It is unconditional love that is "in motion" forever. The Father's love and Christ's love are united and identical. Jesus said in John 14:9 "He who has seen Me has seen the Father." Jesus is the exact reflection of God's tenderness, joy, and heart. His heart is for the "whosoever" (see John 3:16 KJV). Whatever gifting God gives us, it is for the benefit of the "whosoever." The "whosoevers" are your brothers or sisters. However, those people do not know it or act like it. Be pliable to the Holy Spirit's move.

On the other side, within that love, they will love what God loves and will hate what God hates. They will be about doing their Father's business (see Luke 2:49 NKJV), using their gifts, and being trained to use them in their irrevocable calling without repentance (see Rom. 11:29). The Amplified Bible translates Romans 11:29 "for the gifts and the calling of God are irrevocable [for He does not withdraw what He has given, nor does He change His mind about those to whom He gives His grace or to whom He sends His call]." God does not change His mind about what He has foreordained before the foundation of the world for each of His children. Do not be ashamed of what He chose for you. Embrace the teachings that are true to His Word and Spirit, and they will give us life (see 2 Cor. 3:6).

When Generation Zion lives in "agapao," it is a commitment that must be embraced and etched into your spirit. It is also not a light commitment given to His Bride. We, Jesus's body on Earth, must walk-in "agapao." If we partake of the fruit of the Spirit, which is the fruit of the Tree of Life, Jesus Himself. We must, I urge you again, must be committed to loving people as God has loved us. That commitment might also be to expel the person out of the church for a season, which is done now for mainly the wrong reasons (see 1 Corinthians 5).

1 Corinthians 5:12b-13 puts it this way "don't you judge those who are within? But those who are outside, God judges. 'Put away the wicked man from among yourselves.'" Therefore, when we go to a brother or sister in the Lord, the judgment cannot be based on whether we like them or not; we go to them because there is immorality according to the Scriptures. It is called "works of the flesh" (see Gal. 5:19-21 MEV). Remember, that person was also "bought at a price" (1 Cor. 6:20).

Talk with that person with gentleness. Galatians 6:1 says, "brothers, even if a man is caught in some fault, you who are spiritual must restore such a one in a spirit of gentleness; looking to yourself so that you also aren't tempted." Remember, use gentleness as you would talk with yourself. Do not be hard on yourself either. Your Heavenly Father loves you with an everlasting love. His love cannot be worn out.

I want to give you a piece of truth that there is a "t" between the words "immorality" and "immortality." The cross is what restores the brother or sister, which returns them to their "first unconditional love" (see Rev. 2:4). It is what is used to bring the harsh word of correction but draws the raging heart to Jesus.

My grandmother used to say, "the Church is like a hospital" because it is for all people. The sick and the dying, but the attendants, nurses, and doctors are led by the Chief Surgeon General, Jesus Christ. It takes the leading of the five-fold ministry in unison with the Spirit for that local ministry to be wrapped in "agapao" towards His sheep, not ours.

Everyone has a gift and let them be trained up in it. The power gifts of God, which seem so abnormal, will be normal because "it is of the age to come" (Heb. 6:5 NKJV). But the mystery of that age is here and now. Jesus commands that we will do the written things about Him and greater things (see John 14:12). Jesus was of the coming age as it works in us now.

I want to ask you, where are the works Jesus did now? We lost it. God has restored it partially, but we need the greater works. Greater, greater, greater works. The only way to get there is to walk it out in victory by making sure you have nailed your stuff to the cross (see Mark 8:34), then walking it out (see Phil. 2:12), then overcoming it (see 1 John 5:4).

Once we overcome, Jesus promises his overcomers "the fruit of the tree of life, hidden manna to eat, to be clothed in white garments, a white stone with a new name on it, power over the nations, your name not to be blotted out of the Book of Life, your name will be confessed before God the Father and His Angels, not to be hurt by the second death, to be made a pillar in God's temple, the name of His God and His God's city to be written on the overcomer, out of the Heavenly realm the overcomer will HAVE Jesus's NEW NAME **written on them**, to be granted to sit with Jesus on His throne which is next to Yahweh's throne" (see Rev. 2:7, 11, 17, 26, 3:5, 12, and 21).

Then, God says, "He who overcomes shall inherit all things, and I will be his God and he shall be My son" (Rev. 21:7). I want you to notice that the word is "son," not "sons." We are a united body (see Col. 3:15; Gal. 3:28) where there is "neither Jew nor Greek, there is neither slave nor free, there is neither male nor female" (Gal 3:28) where all nations celebrate with Jesus's name written on them (see Rev. 5:9). It is in unity that we overcome. United we stand, divided we fall. Agapao is a united, committed love that makes his *ekklesia* (church) **overcomers**. Overcomers abide in "agapao." My friends, brethren, and submitters to the Holy Spirit's call in your life, please, stand united in "agapao."

"AGAPAO" LOVE is a Commandment

This is the command written by the Holy Spirit in commencement of the Captain of our Salvation, Jesus, in John 15:12 says "this is my commandment to you, that you love [agapao] one another as I have loved [agapao] you."

Christ and the Church – The Mystery of "AGAPAO"

Eph. 5:25-28 defines the relationship of Husband and wife and Christ and the Church with a simple word rendered "agapao." If scribed this way, "husbands, 'agapao' your wives, just as Christ also loved the church and gave Himself for her, that He might sanctify and cleanse her with the washing of water by the word, that He might present her to Himself a glorious church, not having spot or wrinkle or any such thing, but that she should be holy and without blemish. So, husbands ought to 'agapao' their own wives as their own bodies; he who 'agapao' his wife loves himself."

This section has a fourfold meaning:

First, husbands are also a metaphor that points to the Christ portion in our relationship to Jesus. Christ is also the Overcomer of death and the grave, it is unconditional love in a state of perpetual motion or action that goes onward forever.

Second, the purpose of the Generation Zion army of warrior priests is to establish the blood-bought members of the Church by leading them into sanctification or setting themselves apart from the world by making sure they are being watered by the reading of and listening to the written Word, with the Rhema Word (or prophetic word) counseled to them. They are also soaking daily in the very presence and nature of God the Father through the covering of Jesus Christ's blood by the power of the age to come, which is now because we are actually "seated in heavenly *places*" with Christ Jesus (see Eph 1:20 NKJV) for the purpose of Generation Zion going forth and being used to present the **whole** glorious church without any defections of any type.

Third, the established leaders of the Church must not be brutal towards the other members but treat them in holiness.

Finally, the holiness treatment is because that is how Jesus sees us. After all, it is His "agapao" or "love in action" that makes us holy.

Part II – THE GENERATION ZION WARRIOR PRIESTHOOD OF RAINBOW LIGHT

Chapter 4: TO "EN Dü O" (PUT ON)

To "put on" is the Greek verb "en dü o." It means "in the sense of sinking into a garment," Strong's Word Study G1746. We then are commanded to "put on the Lord Jesus Christ" (Rom. 13:14).

The aspect of "putting on" or "en dü o" is by first accepting Jesus in your heart then allowing the Holy Spirit to wrap Himself around you, in you, and to work through you for the purpose of manifesting "agapao" in the "power of his resurrection" (Phil. 3:10). This power works in overflowing according to Acts 2:1-4, which starts with the Baptism of the Holy Spirit.

Generation Zion when working and living together in unity (see Psa. 133:1) there will be a cohesive blend of gifts working in similitude towards a common purpose of being an ambassador of Christ (see 2 Cor. 5:20). This manifestation will happen when they have individually and collectively "en dü o," "agape" love, Christ and the armor of light.

Put On (en dü o) Love

We are told: "put on love, which is the bond of perfection" (Col. 3:14 NKJV) which is moral and spiritual perfectness. It is the glue of holiness and righteousness. The adhesive is the Blood of Jesus. When that glue sticks, it is the perfection of unity of the child of God being in submission to the Holy Spirit, who is in submission to Jesus the Son, who is in submission to God or also known as El Elyon, "The Most High God" through "agapao" (see John 17:22-23).

In Colossians 3:12 when Paul describes us as holy and elect of God, he mentions us as "beloved." The term in the Greek is "agapao." The word for "love" in Colossians 3:14 is "agape." So when we put on "agape"/love we are seen by God as part of His "agapao" or "beloved."

In 1 Thessalonians 1:4 we are called "brethren beloved (agapao)." Jesus is called "the firstborn of many brethren" (Rom. 8:29 NKJV). As Jesus's brothers and sisters we are considered the Christian community of "agapao." How is the possible?

According to Ephesians 1:6 (NKJV), Paul goes on to write that we are "accepted in the beloved (agapao)." Our position in staying holy and blameless before God through Jesus Christ's blood which is through unconditional love/"agape" (see Eph. 1:4).

Generation Zion's commission of putting on "agape" translates them into the Lord's "agapao" community. When translated into this community we then start to walk in the fulness of Christ.

Put On (en dü o) Christ

Another aspect of putting on unconditional love is to "put on Christ" (Gal. 3:27). When you put on Christ, you put on the aspect of the Messiah to the world. You become that part of His body that walks in the realm of the supernatural.

Generation Zion will see the supernatural things that are not normal in their lives first then yours as the Spirit reveals. It is a life walking in victory. It is a life that overcomes challenges. It is a life that perseveres. It is a life of walking in the light of the Lord Jesus Christ.

Put On (en dü o) The Armor of Light

Once you put on the Lord Jesus Christ, the rest of Romans 13:14 (NKJV) comes in where we are to "make no provision for the flesh, to fulfill its lusts," which is called "works of darkness" (Rom. 13:12). We then are told to "put on the armor of light" (Rom. 13:12). That armor is seen and thought of according to a Roman Soldier as described in Ephesians 6:10-18.

When Jesus walked on the Earth, His form of spiritual warfare and victory was through fasting and prayer. Jesus was born a Jew and what was the apex of Judaism during the time of the Jesus that was established during the reign of Solomon tied to? It was the temple.

What does every temple have? They have temple guards. Generation Zion are warrior priests that are submitted to the eternal High Priest Jesus Christ according to the order of the Melchizedekian priesthood (see Heb. 6:20). Jesus has called us to be God the Father's royal priests that is called into His marvelous light. Because we are in the light, we must tell all about it (see Rev. 1:6; 1 Pet. 2:9 Contemporary English Version (CEV)).

The armor of light can also be seen from the military temple priests that walk in God's light. They are referred to in the Old Testament as Gatekeepers or Doorkeepers (see 1 Chr. 9:19 (New International Version (NIV) or New American Standard Bible (NASB)).

I call Generation Zion to come forth into your Godly warrior priesthood mentality. Move forward as the Lord Jesus Christ's priestly guards. Make war through prayer and fasting being clothed with the armor of light!

Chapter 5: THE WARRIOR PRIESTHOOD

Priestly Guards: *šô ʿēr (Sho-Air)*/**Thoo-ro-ros**

Jesus has called us to be a "kingdom of priests" (Rev. 1:5 NASB) which is a reiteration of Exodus 19:6. Our older brother, Peter, calls us "a royal priesthood" (1 Pet. 2:9). If we are then called priests, our type and model from Scripture are based on the Levitical priesthood. Though, let me reiterate this, we are <u>not</u> Levites but, Melchizedekian priests. There are six various types of priests and diversities within the priesthood.

According to Scripture, there are Priests, Priests' Assistants, Singers, Musicians, Gatekeepers or also known as Doorkeepers, and Keepers of the Treasure. Within these services, there are the *šô ʿēr (Sho-Air)* or Door/Gatekeepers of the Spirit realm. What do I mean by that?

Just as false religions have their warriors that guard the temple entrance, so does Elohim as we begin to be a corporate body and become defenders of the Faith, family, and friends. Whoever God puts in our path to protect, then we become Melchizedekian *šô ʿēr aka* Door/Gate-keeper warriors of the Most High God. The Scripture mentions the usage of a Gatekeeper in 1 Chronicles 26:1-19 in the building of the Temple of Solomon.

Solomon initiated the *Šô ʿēr* in 2 Chronicles 8:14 "according to the ordinance of David his father, the divisions of the priests to their service, and the Levites to their offices, to praise and to minister before the priests, (to praise and serve before the priests) as the duty of every day required; the doorkeepers also by their divisions at every gate, for David the man of God had so commanded." Jesus inaugurates us, under the current Melchizedekian priesthood, through His ancestor King David (see Rev. 22:16), to be *Šô ʿēr* (Gatekeepers).

Instructions of the *Šô ʿēr* in the Old Covenant

David and Samuel, the seer, had appointed them, the Šô ʿēr, to their trusted office. The Šô ʿēr and their children

> were chosen to be gatekeepers in the thresholds were two hundred twelve. These were listed by genealogy in their villages, whom David and Samuel the seer ordained in their office of trust. So they and their children had the oversight of the gates of Yahweh's house, even the house of the tent, as guards. On the four sides were the gatekeepers, toward the east, west, north, and south. Their brothers, in their villages, were to come in every seven days from time to time to be with them: for the four chief gatekeepers, who were Levites, were in an office of trust, and were over the rooms and over the treasuries in God's house. They stayed around God's house, because that duty was on them; and to their duty was its opening morning by morning (1 Chr. 9:22-27).

the New Covenant Instructions for the *Šô ʿēr*/Thoo-ro-ros

Jesus gave specific anointings for His Thoo-ro-ros:

1. To keep watch for His coming (see Mark 13:34 New Living Translation (NLT)).
2. Guards the opening of the Gate of the sheep (see John 10:3).

This gate that Jesus enters first is the temple made without hands, our Temple. It is the temple of the Holy Spirit. This is where you, the believer (Generation Zion), must guard yourself against wicked and evil things. As a Temple Warrior, you must protect your mind and make sure you are "bringing every thought into captivity to the obedience of Christ" (2 Cor. 10:5). Attacks will come from every corner of the Earth. They will attack using religious, political, social, and economic traps to keep you off your feet.

Once you are taking thoughts captive you begin renewing them with the Word of God and preparing for the spiritual attacks you must watch for Jesus's coming. It is watching for the times and seasons of His return. It is making sure your lampstand is full and not empty. Being wise and not foolish as you await the Captain of our Salvation's coming.

The Temple Captain

Jesus is called the "Captain of our Salvation" (Heb. 2:10 NKJV). "The captain of the guard saw that every man was alert, chastising a priest if found asleep at his post."[10]

As the writer of Hebrews was speaking to Hebrew Christians, the thought pattern of the Holy Spirit was about the Temple and the Aaronic priesthood versus the Melchizedekian priesthood and the Temple captain and Jesus as the Great Captain.

Because of Salvation in Jesus, the Holy Spirit refreshes our minds to stay awake. Peter instructs us to "be vigilant" or "watchful" (see 1 Pet. 5:8). Why? "Your adversary, the devil, walks around like a roaring lion, seeking whom he may devour" (1 Pet. 5:8)

The Temple Captain says, "watch therefore, for you don't know when the lord of the house is coming, whether at evening, or at midnight, or when the rooster crows, or in the morning; lest coming suddenly he might find you sleeping. What I tell you, I tell all: Watch" (Mark 13:35-37).

He also says it is time to "Awake, awake! Put on your strength, O Zion; Put on your beautiful garments, Jerusalem, the holy city" (Isa. 52:1).

The following portion of the song *REVOLUTION NOW!* was recorded live from the Fire School of Ministry and the Temple Captain declares and roars that "we will fight to the death, worthless idols we detest, let the armies and the roar, holiness to the Lord!"[11]

Chapter 6: THE GARMENT OF RAINBOW LIGHT

As Generation Zion Gatekeepers "Šôʿēr"/"Thoo-ro-ros" who roar with" holiness to the Lord" wears the armor of light. Part of that armor is a garment that is also called a tunic. Whether a warrior or a priest a tunic was always worn.

THE GARMENT OF LIGHT

As this garment is wrapped around you, I want you to envision the King enthroned in the recesses of your heart. Out of your heart I want you to feel His glorious presence of rainbow light filling you from the inside out then wrapping around your whole body.

ISRAEL AND JOSEPH

Genesis 37:3-4 describes how Joseph was loved the most by his father Israel and was given a tunic or robe of many colors. As God loves us and has called each of us by name, we have a spiritual inheritance as sons of Israel. Israel means "Prince with God" or "Prince with El" or "Prince with the Creator of Genesis 1." Israel struggled with the Angel of God, and He told him the meaning of his name, Israel, "for you have fought with God and with men, and have prevailed" (Gen. 32:28). Beloved, we are overcomers. This is a type and shadow of Jesus and us, His Body, that we too go through multiple situations, and we overcome, prevail, and persevere.

Paul called us the "Israel of God" (Gal. 6:16 NKJV), meaning when we stand in the glory of the Cross of Christ, without boasting about circumcision or uncircumcision or in our flesh we walk according to the rule that peace, and mercy (see Gal. 6:15-16 NKJV) will "*be* upon the Israel of God" or those that prevail and overcome. For the Body of Jesus is represented between Israel and Joseph. Israel represents Jesus as the Head, and Joseph represents the Body of Christ or the body of the anointed ones (Generation Zion).

THE GARMENT OF RAINBOW COLORS

As Joseph was the most loved child of his father, Jacob, how much more does our Heavenly Father love us? He has given us the mantle, coat or tunic/garment of many colors of rainbow light. How glorious it is to be arrayed in such a glorious mantle. When we "put on" or *"en dü o"* the Garments of Light we are first clothed with a priestly tunic of many colors.

A tunic is the first garment put on for a priest as instructed by God (see Exo. 28:4; Exo. 28:39-40). The only garments given to the regular priests are tunics and sashes (see Exo. 28:40). The description of the tunic is woven of "fine linen *thread*" (Exo. 28:39 NKJV). From the very beginning, the priestly clothing for the Melchizedekian Generation Zion priests of Jesus Christ is made up of righteous acts (see Rev. 19:8). Meaning all the clothing of the priesthood is righteous before God. Since we have Jesus's righteousness, we thus are clothed in righteousness.

God declares that we are "a royal priesthood" (1 Pet. 2:9) which was first spoken of in Exodus 19:6 that God declared to the nation of Israel, "you shall be to me a kingdom of priests" and "you will be called Yahweh's priests" (Isa. 61:6) and "he made us to be a Kingdom, priests to his God and Father" (Rev. 1:6) "a priest forever in the order of Melchizedek" (see Psa. 110:4; Heb. 5:6, 7:21).

Jesus desires a relationship with His Melchizedekian ministers that they go to Him and the Father. Our Father is known by many names, and during the times of the Old Testament, He has been revealed as El Elyon or the God Most High (see Gen. 14:18) or called the "high and lofty One" (Isa. 57:15). Our ministry to God is a Heavenly priesthood to His Majesty on High who is the Lofty One who sits beyond time and space.

Chapter 7: THE PURPOSE OF THE GARMENT OF RAINBOW LIGHT

Psalm 45:13-14 describes the royal King's daughter who symbolizes the Bride of Christ. She is "brought" and "wrapped in" robes of many colors. This is a love psalm between the Messiah and His Bride. The daughter's description begins by being brought to the King singularly, who is God the Father, and then mentions robes.

The robes signify majesty, and then being plural means many people. I want to reiterate "for as the body is one, and has many members, and all the members of the body, being many, are one body; so also is Christ...for the body is not one member, but many" (1 Cor. 12:12, 14). This psalm shows that though the Bride consists of many people, she is seen as one person. A corporate body of Christians in love with Jesus, their Head, and Bridegroom. They are united to Jesus through submission to Him, in totality: body, soul, and spirit. Like Generation Zion is composed of multiple generations in one united generation whose robes symbolize a single garment of rainbow light.

WRAPPED IN A MULTICOLORED GARMENT OF LIGHT

Generation Zion priests are wrapped in God's multicolored garment of light represented as Joseph's coat or tunic of many colors. When it is placed on each individual, it represents the nations and people we are to minister to. For "out of every tribe, language, people, and nation" (Rev. 5:9), God has called us for the purpose of reigning on the Earth (see Rev. 5:10). When we are sent forth, we are enwrapped with God's tender mercies from the beginning. "But God, being rich in mercy, for his great love with which he loved us, even when we were dead through our trespasses, made us alive together with Christ—by grace you have been saved — and raised us up with him, and made us to sit with him in the heavenly places in Christ Jesus, that in the ages to come he might show the exceeding riches of his grace in kindness toward us in Christ Jesus" (Eph. 2:4-7).

In the ages to come through His mercy, He has shown us that there are great riches to come because of His love and unmerited favor for all that accept Jesus, which qualifies us to behold His majesty in the ages to come.

In the series *STUDIES IN THE BEAUTY OF GOD*, Mike Bickle writes *The Emerald Rainbow: The God of Tender Mercy (Rev 4:3) Section I. THE GOD OF THE EMERALD RAINBOW* describes the mercy we receive through the emerald rainbow:

> we receive mercy based on what Jesus did on the cross, not on what we have accomplished. Jesus, the innocent One, became guilty so that the guilty ones who believe in Him may become innocent. God's mercy forgives us and assures that what would disqualify us from our destiny is removed,
>
> if we will receive God's grace (2 Cor. 5:17-21 NKJV)."[12]

Continuing in Mike Bickle's *STUDIES IN THE BEAUTY OF GOD*, he writes *The Emerald Rainbow: The God of Tender Mercy (Rev 4:3) Section II. ALL OF GOD'S WORKS ARE SURROUNDED WITH MERCY* about the description of the rainbow that surrounds God's throne:

> the rainbow around God's Throne completely encircles it. In other words, God's mercy surrounds all the activity that proceeds from His Throne. John used the rare Greek word for rainbow (*"iris"*) instead of the common one (*toxon*) to point out how it makes a full circle (instead of a semicircle) around God's Throne.[13]

Ezekiel saw God's throne with a rainbow around the throne "The Throne...with the appearance of a man high above it...The appearance of a rainbow...was the appearance of the brightness all around it (Throne in v26). This was the appearance of the likeness of the glory of the Lord" (Eze 1:26, 28 NKJV). Again, the rainbow is around God's throne for "he who trusts in the Lord, mercy shall surround him" (Psa. 32:10 NKJV). "All the paths of the Lord are mercy and truth, to such as keep His covenant" (Psa. 25:10 NKJV).

THE SYMBOLISM OF THE RAINBOW

The colors of the rainbow that God means for us to be enveloped in are in this order: red, orange, yellow, green, blue, indigo, and violet (purple). The rainbow is made up of three primary colors: red, yellow, and blue, while the secondary colors are orange, green, and violet. These numbers total six, whose number is associated with humanity. Indigo is between blue and violet, making it seven or the number of completion and rest.

The order in which the rainbow flows is from top to bottom as the "veil of the temple was ripped from top to bottom" (see Mat. 27:51; Mark 15:38), which symbolizes your flesh being crucified through a process to the glory of God's royalty. The rainbow colors represent the reflection of God's love toward us, presence, glory, and light. For all the colors are birthed from the mind of God and created in our physical world through Jesus Christ (see Eph. 3:9).

Revelation 4:2-3 describes the heavenly realm of God where there is "a throne set in heaven, and one sitting on the throne that looked like a jasper stone and a sardius. There was a rainbow around the throne, like an emerald to look at." The jasper is described as a pure transparent "diamond-like" stone "clear as crystal" (Rev. 21:11).

Mike Bickle teaches:

> "God covers Himself with a multicolored garment of light
> that shines forth with the colors of jasper (crystal), sardius

(red), emerald (green), and the various colors of the rainbow.[14]

That rainbow ("*iris*") is also described with an emerald glow. Why emerald? Mike Bickle explains:

> Emerald green speaks of life (vegetation). God's beautiful personality is seen in how He relates to His people with great kindness and tenderness. This emerald rainbow of mercy encompasses all the plans and actions that issue forth from God's throne. His mercies cover all that He does, and it endures forever (see Psa. 103:17; Psa. 145:9)."[15]

When wrapped in the "iris" it shows us that each Christian in Generation Zion must be merciful and exemplify *agapao* (love that is continually in action or motion). We are to imitate Christ (see 1 Cor. 11:1) for "blessed *are* the people who know the joyful sound! They walk, O Lord in the light of Your countenance" (Psa. 89:15 NKJV) and "walk-in....the light of life" (John 8:12). Again, I say, "we walk in the light, as he is in the light, we have fellowship with one another, and the blood of Jesus Christ, his Son, cleanses us from all sin" (1 John 1:7).

THE SYMBOLISM of THE RAINBOW IN FIRE

The rainbow is reflected in the fire of God's pure light and fire. For "the Light of Israel will be for a fire, and his Holy One for a flame" (Isa. 10:17). The light from the Holy One is reflected in the Overcomer, which flows out of the heart of God and is reflected in the sea of glass, which is mixed with fire (see Rev. 15:2).

In science, there are also many levels of fire that are separated by the rainbow. Starting at the top to the bottom is red down to purple/violet. Violet is the hottest of all fires, which glow at approximately 71,000-degrees Fahrenheit. It glows about 8.4 times brighter than our Sun.[16] God is mentioned as a "consuming fire" (see Deut. 4:24; Heb.

12:29) in which we as His ministers are to be walking iridescent fires (see Psa. 104:4; Heb. 1:7).

Fire is also a representation of God's purification process. In Malachi 3:2, God is called a refiner's fire. Why does He refine us? What is the point? That through "various trials, the genuineness of your faith…that the proof of your faith, which is more precious than gold that perishes even though it is tested by fire, may be found to result in praise, glory, and honor at the revelation of Jesus Christ — whom, not having known, you love. In him, though now you don't see him, yet believing, you rejoice greatly with joy that is unspeakable and full of glory,receiving the result of your faith, the salvation of your souls" (1 Pet. 1:6-9).

We are to reflect this multicolor light to the world as the Body of Christ because Jesus said of Himself, "as long as I am in the world, I AM the light of the world" (John 9:5 NKJV), and when Jesus gave us the Holy Spirit who came in His name (see John 14:26). He became the fulfillment of Matthew 5:14 where He declares us as "the light of the world." It also represents the Power of God. This power is not to control the things of this world but to pray for the things "that pertain to life and godliness, through the knowledge of him who called us by his own glory and virtue, by which he has granted to us his precious and exceedingly great promises; that through these you may become partakers of the divine nature, having escaped from the corruption that is in the world by lust" (2 Pet. 1:3-4).

When Jesus was in the Garden, He prays to our Father, "glorify Me together with Yourself, with the glory which I had with You before the world was" (John 17:5 NKJV) "and the glory which You gave Me I have given them, that they may be one just as We are one" (John 17:22 NKJV underline mine).

This glory is the light and fire of His multi-colored garment of mercy. Let the path of the Lord's light shine brighter and brighter until the perfect day of His coming comes (see Pro. 4:18). Generation Zion imitate God's rainbow light/fire of mercy. I dare you. Do you accept this challenge? I dare you to walk in the light of your fire now (see Isa. 50:11 NASB). Jesus wants a deeper relationship with you through the power of the Holy Spirit. This is the dynamite or Dunamis power that gives you resurrection life whose authority or covering is represented in the multicolored garment of light.

I invite you to read on and hear what the Spirit is saying in these last days about Generation Zion and the colors designed for warfare. Each color is designed to equip us to another realm of God's love and power where we do battle in the heavenlies.

Chapter 8: THE GARMENT OF RAINBOW LIGHT: THE COLOR WHITE

Melissa Tumino, in *THE ULTIMATE GUIDE TO THE COLORS IN THE BIBLE,* writes "that the colors of the rainbow come from the white light."[17] To put on the light, you have put it on first spiritually where the light "abolished death and brought life and immortality" (2 Tim. 1:10). Then at the physical appearance of the King, you will put it physically on "for this perishable body must become imperishable, and this mortal must put on immortality. But when this perishable body will have become imperishable, and this mortal will have put on immortality, then what is written will happen: 'Death is swallowed up in victory'" (1 Cor. 15:53-54). Victory to the overcoming bride!

Yes, victory to the King of kings and His victorious warrior bride (Generation Zion)! This warrior bride is clothed in white garments (see Rev. 3:5).

The Color of White

The meaning of the color white is where all colors come out of. White is defined as coming from God and Jesus. It is where we receive His righteousness, and holiness. It is where we are cleansed from sin and iniquity. We then can live a life of purity."[18]

In Psalm 104:1-2, God is described as "clothed with honor and majesty. He covers himself with light as with a garment." showing that all honor, then majesty go to Him and Him alone. We honor Him, for He is holy. The declaration "I, Yahweh your God, am holy" (Lev. 19:2b) declares this and that we are to be holy ourselves (see Lev. 19:2a), and this is reiterated that "he who called you is holy, you yourselves also be holy in all of your behavior; because it is written, "You shall be holy; for I am holy" (1 Pet. 1:15-16).

Generation Zion is praising and worshiping the true living God, for it is written, "exalt Yahweh, our God. Worship at his holy hill, for Yahweh, our God, is holy!" (Psa. 99:9). The place where we worship is holy.

I want us to pray this that no matter what is going on in life, we implore our Great King to "remember Your congregation, *which* You have purchased of old, the tribe of Your inheritance, *which* You have redeemed — This Mount Zion where You have dwelt" (Psa. 74:2 NKJV). For "those who trust in Yahweh are as Mount Zion, which can't be moved, but remains forever" (Psa. 125:1). This is from the songs of ascent. They are sung when ascending to Jerusalem during the Feast of Tabernacles.

This is a time of prophetic teaching that "the tabernacle of God *is* with men, and He will dwell with them, and they shall be His people. God Himself will be with them *and be* their God" (Rev. 21:3 NKJV). This is literal and figurative. Through the Holy Spirit, God dwells in us, so He is literally tabernacling with us, and yet in the future, He will tabernacle in a complete physical form that every eye shall behold. God says, "My tabernacle also shall be with them; indeed, I will be their God, and they shall be My people" (Eze. 37:27 NKJV). Dry bones, tabernacle with God as fully dressed and clothed in spiritual garments of light.

As we ascend to God, we do it because it is written, "God the Holy One is sanctified in righteousness" (Isa. 5:16). Hallowed is to praise Him all of us who are His people. For "Yahweh is righteous" (Exo. 9:27). "*He is* the Rock, His work *is* perfect; For all His ways *are* justice, A God of truth and without injustice; Righteous and upright *is* He" (Deut. 32:4 NKJV).

Because of our faith in Jesus Christ, it "is accounted for righteousness" (Rom. 4:5b). This same Jesus is who Abraham looked to, who is our forefather. Because of this righteousness and being children of faith, we have hope because Jesus purifies those that want to be pure because He is pure (see 1 John 3:3). Through this purity we are holy. It is written, "Jesus Christ who gave himself for us, that he might redeem us from all iniquity, and purify for himself a people for his own possession, zealous for good works" (Tit. 2:13-14).

This purification made us His "own special people," my friends, brothers, and sisters of Generation Zion in Christ Jesus "What God has cleansed you must not call common" (Acts 10:15 NKJV). We are not common but "His special people" (1 Pet. 2:9 NKJV). It is written and fulfilled when we are "turned white: he is clean" (Lev. 13:13). This passage of Leviticus describes leprosy. Were we not leprous to the Lord? Were we not unclean? The Lord has declared us clean!

PUTTING ON LIGHT

As we put on Christ, I want to remind you of the following: It was "Jesus...[who] brought them up into a high mountain by themselves. He was changed before them. His face shone like the sun, and his garments became as white as the light" (Mat. 17:1-2). What did Jesus do? He led the apostles up the high mountain. As we ascend Mount Zion, we become transfigured like Him. He clothed Himself "with light as with a garment" (Psa. 104:2).

When we put on Christ Jesus, we put on His light. Because our robes are washed in the blood of the Lamb, they have been made white (see Rev. 7:14). This garment flows down to the feet (see Rev. 1:13 NKJV) and gives us authority over the enemy (see Rom. 16:20). The Son of Man says, "Don't be afraid. I am the first and the last, and the Living one. I was dead, and behold, I am alive forever and ever. Amen. I have the keys of Death and of Hades (or the unseen demonic realm)" (Rev. 1:17-18).

God states that My light reveals and exposes the hidden things in your life (see John 3:20). This is not always about correction but love (agapao) and unhiding those who are "hidden with Christ in God" (Col. 3:3). When wrapped in His light, we access God's purity, His

Word, and eternal life that does not corrupt. We are seen before El Shaddai/God Almighty, as true sons of the Living God. Light consumes us, and it is His light that reveals the colors of the fire.

That fire burns, drives, and consumes us to be servants of fire (see Heb. 1:7). That fire is the Word in us because we are the lamp contained in Earthen vessels, the Glory of the Only Begotten Lord Jesus that lights our path (see Psa. 119:105). Jesus said, "I AM the light of the world" (John 8:12 NKJV), and He calls out His body as "the light of the world" (Mat. 5:14).

Jesus also said to the individual "He who follows me will not walk in the darkness, but will have the light of life" (John 8:12) for "I lead you out of darkness" (see Job 29:3). He guides us through the darkness or the unseen realm of death to the seen realm of the living light. As we seek Jesus, He comes forth out of our hearts to reveal the glory of God as the face of Jesus Christ to the world (see 2 Cor. 4:6).

The "light shines on the righteous and joy on the upright in heart" (Psa. 97:11 NIV) because that light shines into your being out flows love and grace. God is gracious and full of compassion, and righteousness (see Psa. 116:5 NIV). "The path of the righteous is like the light of dawn that shines brighter and brighter until the full day" (Pro. 4:18 NASB), meaning since we are born again and continue to pursue Jesus's light and mercy, we continue to shine brighter and brighter in His agape love. From agape, we then move into agapao, then move between agapao and agape and agape and agapao depending on the moment until the full day of maturity is at hand.

THE RIGHTEOUS RECEIVE CHRIST'S LIGHT

This light is given to the righteous. It is because of this light we are righteous. Rejoice My righteous ones for now "the Lord *is* righteous within her" (Zeph. 3:5a NASB) the Church, His spouse, "He will do no injustice. Every morning He brings His justice to light" (Zeph. 3:5 NASB). Though we go through trials, we need not fear during these unknown times. We are the Overcoming Generation Zion!

The Holy Spirit says:

"Be patient. Know I AM who I say I AM. I do not change! Though things go upside down, know I AM in control. Do not be afraid, do not fret, and be strong and courageous. My Shalom, I give you, My holy city, My Beloved ones, My chosen Generation "ZION." I live or dwell in you. I shame you not. But hold you upright during these perilous times.

"'The unjust know no shame' (Zeph. 3:5e) because I am not with them in protection, but with you. I AM your solid rock, Jesus, who cares and loves you. I want the best for you. I uphold you with My mighty hand.

"Again, stay in the light for I Am the light (see John 8:12) that guides you. Do not go right or left. Trust in My Word, My Rhema, My Scriptures testify all about My Kingdom. Proclaim this 'The Kingdom of Heaven is at hand' (Mat. 10:7) and is here now among you and in you. Trust My true and faithful servants as torch and light-bearers. I proclaim My secrets through trusted apostles and prophets (see Eph. 3:5). These are refined for this day for My light shines. Arise, shine, wake up, trust in the unveiling of My Spirit for the unveiling of your circumcised heart for protection of your true righteous nature that when aligned with Me, I will be able to move Heaven and Earth for the building of My Body and My Christ.

"I lead you to Mount Zion and the tabernacle of meeting where I reside in you which is revealed in My light and truth (see Psa. 43:3). As My servant, David proclaimed, 'Yahweh is my light and my salvation. Whom shall I fear? Yahweh is the strength of my life. Of whom shall I be afraid?' (Psa.

27:1), for I AM 'the light of the morning, when the sun rises' (2 Sam. 23:4) out of the darkness. I call you out mentally, emotionally, spiritually free," says the God of Angel Armies and the Sabaoth.

"For through you, they see Me. Because of My resurrection, I fulfill what is written that those 'who walked in darkness and lived in the land of the shadow of death, upon them a light' (Isa. 9:2a-b NKJV), which is 'you in Me and I in you' (see John 17:23) 'has shined' (Isa. 9:2). Let My testimony that shines through the blood, the water, and the oil. They represent My death and resurrection, being washed in the river of life, and being sealed with My Spirit, which guarantees your inheritance (see Eph. 1:13-14) of the Kingdom.

"I have called you 'children of light' (John 12:36) 'and children of the day' (see 1 The. 5:5), for I have given you 'the Good News of the glory of Christ, who is the image of God' to shine upon you (see 2 Cor. 4:4) which shines out of your hearts (see 2 Cor. 4:6). For I have called you out from 'a crooked and perverse generation, among whom you shine as lights in the world' (Phil. 2:15)."

For this very reason, we are part of the armies of heaven; we are clothed in fine linen, white and clean, following Him on White horses (see Rev. 19:14). This light comes from God and allows us to be seated with Jesus, who sits on a stable and unshakeable throne. This Jasper stone allows the rainbow of God to shine through us and reveals the beginning of the mystery of Joseph's 'tunic of many colors' (Gen. 37:3) or garment of rainbow light. For out of His light, we see true light (see Psa. 36:9), for "light dwells with Him" (Dan. 2:22). "Let your light shine before men, that they may see your good works and glorify your Father who is in heaven" (Mat. 5:16).

Chapter 9: THE GARMENT OF RAINBOW LIGHT: THE COLOR RED

Red in its purest essence according to the Hebrew word, is translated as "mankind." It is the word is "Oudem" or red clay from which we get the word "Adam" and is also known as scarlet.[19]

When discussing the beginning process of identification at the beginning of our redemption this scarlet color must be identified with our sinfulness and self-righteousness which is to be compared and thought of as "menstrual rags" (see Isa. 1:18, 64:6). After your sin is identified, the red/scarlet color then represents the blood of Christ that "cleanses us from all sin" (1 John 1:7), purifies us from all sin (see Heb. 9:22 NKJV), redeems us (see 1 Pet. 1:18-19), and sanctifies your body, soul, and spirit (see 1 The. 5:23).[20]

It is a primary color mentioned in the Tabernacle of Moses (see Exo. 26:1, 27:16, 28:6; Num. 4:1-13).[21] Melissa Tumino, in *THE ULTIMATE GUIDE TO THE COLORS IN THE BIBLE,* defines the color red in the tabernacle as the basis of our relationship to Jesus as the Son of Man and the Last Adam (see John 8:28; 1 Cor. 15:45).[22] When God starts to manifest and dwell in our tabernacle, it speaks of our relation to the blood being in us and as the Bride of Christ that it is a sign of wealth that is of a virtuous woman according to Proverbs 31:21 (NKJV) "for all her household *is* clothed with scarlet."

In the book of the Revelation of Jesus Christ, Jesus is represented as the sardius stone in Revelation 4:2-3. Once we can identify Him as seated on the throne of authority and power, with the knowledge and belief that He will come back in the natural, we can wage warfare in the natural realm with His return. For now, our warfare is in the Spirit realm. The color red represents Jesus as the leader of a unified army. This Generation Zion army is made up of multiple battalions of celestial and terrestrial bodies following Him into war[23] as indicated in the following passages:

Jesus – The Man of War

Who *is* this who comes from Edom, with dyed garments from Bozrah, This *One who is* glorious in His apparel, Traveling in the greatness of His strength? — "I who speak in righteousness, mighty to save." Why *is* <u>Your apparel red, And Your garments like one who treads in the winepress?</u> "I have trodden the winepress alone, and from the peoples no one *was* with Me. For I have trodden them in My anger, and trampled them in My fury; Their blood is sprinkled upon My garments, and I have stained all My robes (Isa. 63:1-3 NKJV underline mine).

<u>He *was* clothed with a robe dipped in blood</u>, and His name is called The Word of God. And the armies in heaven, clothed in fine linen, white and clean, followed Him on white horses. Now out of His mouth goes a sharp sword, that with it He should strike the nations. And He Himself will rule them with a rod of iron. <u>He Himself treads the winepress of the fierceness and wrath of Almighty God</u> (Rev. 19:13-15 NKJV underline mine).

The Church and Angels – His Army

The prophet Nahum declares that "the shield of his mighty men is made red, the valiant men are in scarlet" (Nah. 2:3).[24]

The color red symbolizes in the rainbow garment of light that the old man who is made out of the first Adam (see 1 Cor. 15:47), who was laden with sin and self-righteousness, has been cleansed of all sin, purified or set apart from the world by the blood of Jesus Christ or the second Adam (see 1 Cor. 15:47) in which we "shall also bear the image of the heavenly *Man*" (1 Cor. 15:49 NKJV). Which is spirit, soul, and body who robes us with a heavenly treasure (see Mat. 6:19-21) which is "an incorruptible and undefiled inheritance that doesn't fade away, reserved in Heaven for you" (1 Pet. 1:4) right now in which we are led by our Commander and Chief Jesus Christ who leads us to war Generation "ZION!"

Chapter 10: THE GARMENT OF RAINBOW LIGHT: THE COLOR ORANGE

Orange is never referenced in the Bible. In the garment of rainbow light Orange is to be defined and revealed through other symbols in Scripture that are orange.[25]

In Ezekiel 24:6 and Matthew 6:19-20, the colors are associated with <u>scum and rust</u>, which are defined as corruption. Ezekiel 24:6 is written:

> O Wherefore thus saith the Lord God; Woe to the bloody city, to the pot whose <u>scum</u> is therein, and whose scum is not gone out of it! Bring it out piece by piece; let no lot fall upon it (KJV underline mine).

> O Don't lay up treasures for yourselves on the earth, where moth and <u>rust</u> consume, and where thieves break through and steal;but lay up for yourselves treasures in heaven, where neither moth nor <u>rust</u> consume, and where thieves don't break through and steal (Mat. 6:19-20 underline mine).

Another aspect and view of orange is associated with rebellion or scum iron.[26] Iron is a mixture of red and yellow hues with brown tinges[27] as described in Jeremiah 6:28. God the Father states about His rebellious people that "they *are* all stubborn rebels...*They are* bronze and iron." Orange can then be represented as clay or Earthen vessels.[28] "When the vessel that he made of the clay was marred in the hand of the potter, he made it again another vessel, as seemed good to the potter to make it" (Jer. 18:4). "Or hasn't the potter a right over the clay, from the same lump to make one part a vessel for honor, and another for dishonor?" (Rom. 9:21).

TRANSITION FROM RED TO ORANGE: SAVED TO BUILD UP AND PROTECT THE HEAVENLY TREASURE

In the rainbow garment of light, the color red is manifested and transitioned into the color orange. It is where scum and rust of the corruption of sinful life should not be treasured up in yourself, Generation "ZION." Allow your treasures to be heavenly that do not corrupt with scum and rust.

The old nature was once stubborn and rebellious, but now you are being formed as clay vessels for honor who were once clay vessels of dishonor for "it shall come to pass in the place where it was said to them, 'You *are* not My people,' There they shall be called sons of the living God" (Rom. 9:26 NKJV). For this purpose, "He might make known the riches of His glory on the vessels of mercy, which He had prepared beforehand for glory" (Rom. 9:23 NKJV). You have become orange earthen clay vessels of mercy and honor. Children and friends of God who know that they are daily being refined into the image of the Lord Jesus Christ.

Chapter 11: THE GARMENT OF RAINBOW LIGHT: The Color Yellow

Yellow is represented in Scripture as either yellow and/or amber.[29] It represents the anointing oil and God's glory and His presence.[30]

In Exodus 30:22-25, it is written:

> Moreover Yahweh spoke to Moses, saying, "Also take fine spices: of liquid myrrh, five hundred shekels; and of fragrant cinnamon half as much, even two hundred and fifty; and of fragrant cane, two hundred and fifty; and of cassia five hundred, according to the shekel of the sanctuary; and a hin of olive oil. You shall make it into a holy anointing oil, a perfume compounded after the art of the perfumer: it shall be a holy anointing oil.

Olive oil is naturally a yellow hue.[31]

Then it is written in 1 Samuel 16:13 "Then Samuel took the horn of oil and anointed him in the middle of his brothers. Then Yahweh's Spirit came mightily on David from that day forward." The anointing oil is associated with the Holy Spirit.

In Ezekiel 1:4 (NKJV), God's glory is coming out of the clouds as described by prophet Ezekiel "then I looked, and behold, a whirlwind was coming out of the north, a great cloud with raging fire engulfing itself; and brightness *was* all around it and <u>radiating out of its midst like the color of amber</u>, out of the midst of the fire."

In Ezekiel 1:27 (NKJV underline mine) God's physical manifest body is described "from the appearance of His waist and upward I saw, as it were, the <u>color of amber</u> with the appearance of fire all around within it" and Ezekiel 8:2 (NKJV underline mine) "from His waist and upward, like the appearance of brightness, like <u>the color of amber</u>."

TRANSITION FROM ORANGE TO YELLOW: TRANSFORMATION FROM THE OLD TO YOUR NEW NATURE

In the rainbow garment of light, the color orange is manifested and transitioned into yellow, you start to function as a priest in the unchanging and eternal Melchizedek priesthood (see Heb. 7:11-27). This is when the anointing of the Holy Spirit starts to operate through your giftings that are irrevocable (see Rom. 11:29), and you begin to submit more and go further in God. The revelation of your gifts begins to grow once you start growing in your relationship with the Father, Son, and Holy Spirit. Each one serves a different purpose in your life relating to how your gifting functions.

The Triune-God who the Father heads decides your gifts. Jesus is the way to activate your gifts functioning correctly by applying His blood in your life, which comprises your mind, will, and emotions. The Holy Spirit sees the blood, which activates the anointing of your gifts using your mind, will, emotions, and five senses.

The more time you spend in prayer and reading your word, the more you can be used in your giftings. Get the training, practice, then be released by a ministry that supports your gifts.

"For however many are the promises of God, in him is the "Yes." Therefore also through him is the "Amen", to the glory of God through us. Now he who establishes us with you in Christ and anointed us is God, who also sealed us, and gave us the down payment of the Spirit in our hearts" (2 Cor. 1:20-22). "As for you, the anointing which you received from him remains in you, and you don't need for anyone to teach you. But as his anointing teaches you concerning all things, and is true, and is no lie, and even as it taught you, you will remain in him" (1 John 2:27).

Generation Zion must live in the anointing because the Holy Spirit uses men and women to teach. The establishment of the Naioth of prophets or school of the prophets (see 1 Sam. 19:18-24) has been since the times of Samuel, if not earlier. We learn by using concordances, going to Bible colleges and regular schools to learn to read, write, arithmetic, etc. The "Holy Spirit is the one who guides us into all truth" (see John 16:13) or learn to discern the truth through schooling, which may entail the "school of hard knocks and rocks."

Chapter 12: THE GARMENT OF RAINBOW LIGHT: THE COLOR GREEN

Green is represented in Scripture as God's rest, mercy, life or growth, and fruitfulness.[32]

The Scriptures about God's rest are defined as "He makes me lie down in green pastures. He leads me beside still waters" (Psa. 23:2) and gives us "rest in the day of trouble" (Hab. 3:16 NKJV). God stated that the Sabbath or day of rest "is a sign between me and the children of Israel forever; for in six days Yahweh made heaven and earth, and on the seventh day he rested, and was refreshed" (Exo. 31:17). The Lord "shows mercy to His anointed" (Psa. 18:50 NKJV), for we praise the Lord, for His mercy endures forever (see 2 Chr. 7:3 NKJV).

For life and growth are kindled in Scripture that "Yahweh called your name, 'A green olive tree, beautiful with goodly fruit'" (Jer. 11:16) "All the trees of the field will know that I, Yahweh, have brought down the high tree, have exalted the low tree, have dried up the green tree, and have made the dry tree flourish. "'I, Yahweh, have spoken and have done it.'"" (Eze. 17:24). For Job said, "the Spirit of God has made me, and the breath of the Almighty gives me life" (Job 33:4). Our Lord Jesus Christ said "it is the Spirit who gives life; the flesh profits nothing. The words that I speak to you are spirit, and *they* are life" (John 6:63 NKJV). Jesus also spoke that "I have come that they may have life, and that they may have it more abundantly" (John 10:10).

Out of life comes fruitfulness which is demonstrated and hidden in your heart that oh Generation "ZION." The following Scriptures should go forth from your heart:

It was the first commandment given in Scripture to the first Adam and Eve by God saying bless them, and go forth, "be fruitful, multiply, fill the earth, and subdue it. Have dominion over the fish of the sea, over the birds of the sky, and over every living thing that moves on the earth" (Gen 1:28). As part of the beginning of dominion the Scriptures define our first abode that "for as in Adam all die, so also in Christ all will be made alive" (1 Cor. 15:22). It is out of the dominion that Jesus Christ gave us that we can be made alive and His firstfruits.

THE ORDER OF FIRSTFRUITS

"But each one in his own order: Christ the firstfruits, afterward those *who are* Christ's at His coming" (1 Cor. 15:23 NKJV). As we start to go from our position in the first Adam, our natural man, we begin to progress to becoming Jesus Christ's firstfruits, the spiritual man here on Earth now. "So also it is written, "The first man, Adam, became a living soul." The last Adam became a life-giving spirit. However that which is spiritual isn't first, but that which is natural, then that which is spiritual" (1 Cor. 15:45-46). "But each one in his own order: Christ the firstfruits, afterward those *who are* Christ's at His coming" (1 Cor. 15:23 NKJV). The "coming," Paul was talking about was His coming back to Earth, but for us to be His firstfruits, we must allow Him to come and minister in our hearts for us to be His firstfruits.

Once you understand the spiritual, you start to bear the fruit of the Spirit, which "the fruit of the Spirit is in all goodness and righteousness and truth" (Eph. 5:9). This fruit that is born is "of the righteous [which] is a tree of life" (Pro. 11:30).

The Holy Spirit wants to iterate that "as your fruit is bearing from the tree of life and your position that 'the ones...having heard the word with a noble and good heart, keep *it* and bear fruit with patience'" (Luk. 8:15 NKJV).

The watering of that tree and the fruit of life is from "a pure river of water of life, clear as crystal, proceeding from the throne of God and of the Lamb.In the middle of its street, and on either side of the river, *was* the tree of life, which bore twelve fruits, each *tree* yielding its fruit every month. The leaves of the tree *were* for the healing of the nations" (Rev. 22:1-2 NKJV).

Please receive this "He who has an ear, let him hear what the Spirit says to the assemblies. To him who overcomes I will give to eat from the tree of life, which is in the Paradise of my God" (Rev. 2:7).

TRANSITION FROM YELLOW TO GREEN: BEARING A MERCIFUL LIFE OF FIRSTFRUITS

In the rainbow garment of light, the color yellow is manifested and transitioned into the color green, showing God's mercy because God shows Generation Zion mercy. He had a mercy seat or "mercy throne," which sat on top and in between the two cherubim of the Ark of the Covenant or Testimony (see Exo. 25:17-21). Hebrews 8:5 tells us that Moses made the Ark and the Mercy Seat from the pattern shown to him of the Heavenly realms. The tabernacle and its ornaments made by Moses were mere copies and shadows of those in the Father's throne room.

For in mercy, the throne of Jesus Christ is established, and the One who sits on it in truth, in the tabernacle of David (see Isa. 16:5 NKJV), which, has no veil for the people of David. We are his spiritual descendants through Jesus Christ, for David worshipped God with everything he had to the point of his clothes falling off unashamedly (see 2 Sam. 6:20). Jesus's throne of judgment is for those that seek justice and hastening righteousness (see Isa. 16:5). We are told to go "with confidence, so that we may receive mercy and find grace to help us in our time of need" (Heb. 4:16 NIV).

Once that mercy is put on us, we can rest there, spending time in prayer and a day to recuperate from 6 days of working to restart our week rejuvenated. It is necessary to not be harsh taskmasters in the Spirit or physical realms.

For God wants to "teach us to count our days, that we may gain a heart of wisdom" (Psa. 90:12) for "to Him who by wisdom made the heavens, for His mercy *endures* forever" (Psa. 136:5 NKJV) so that we may incline our ears to wisdom and apply wisdom to our hearts for understanding (see Pro. 2:2). To gain knowledge, there must be understanding which is to fear Yahweh (see Pro. 1:7), for "if any of you lacks wisdom, let him ask of God, who gives to all liberally and without reproach, and it will be given to him" (Jas. 1:5). That "the wisdom that is from above is first pure, then peaceful, gentle, reasonable, full of mercy and good fruits, without partiality, and without hypocrisy" (Jas. 3:17).

He has granted us time to live in mercy and tenderness, for our "days are like grass" (see Psa. 103:15). "All flesh is like grass... The grass withers, the flower fades; but the word of our God stands forever" (Isa. 40:6-8). Which shows us however, we are not yet physically eternal; God is. His promises will stand. His promises say, "when he is revealed, we will be like him; for we will see him just as he is" (1 John 3:2), for He gives life abundantly (see John 10:10). An abundant life now! Though you may not be rich with money, you can now have an abundant life in unconditional love!

Jesus does tell us to "lay our treasures in heaven" (Mat. 6:20) or in the heavenly realm because Ephesians 2:20-22 tells us that the Church is "built on the foundation of the apostles and prophets, Christ Jesus himself being the chief cornerstone; in whom the whole building, fitted together, grows into a holy temple in the Lord; in whom you also are built together for a habitation of God in the Spirit."

The Holy Spirit will take residence if we allow Him to become the chief resident. We get to have His dwelling or living quarters inside us. The abundant life is that we can host the Holy Spirit and become a living tabernacle of God with the indwelling of the Triune God through the power of the Holy Spirit of the age to come, which is now, because we are seated in the heavenly places (see Eph. 2:6). We celebrate the Feast of Tabernacles during this age by allowing the Holy Spirit to tabernacle with us.

The Feast of Tabernacles or Sukkot is a festival that is to be kept, "it will happen that everyone who is left of all the nations that came against Jerusalem will go up from year to year to worship the King, Yahweh of Armies, and to keep the feast of booths. It will be, that whoever of all the families of the earth doesn't go up to Jerusalem to worship the King, Yahweh of Armies, on them there will be no rain" (Zech. 14:16-17).

When we tabernacle with Jesus now, we present to Him our firstfruits "it shall be, when you have come in to the land which Yahweh your God gives you for an inheritance, possess it, and dwell in it...now, behold, I have brought the first of the fruit of the ground, which you, Yahweh, have given me." You shall set it down before Yahweh your God, and worship before Yahweh your God" (Deut. 26:1, 10). "These are those who follow the Lamb wherever he goes. These were redeemed by Jesus from among men, the first fruits to God and to the Lamb.In their mouth was found no lie, for they are blameless" (Rev. 14:4-5) for "that it is the firstfruits...the ministry of the saints" (1 Cor. 16:15 NKJV), which is "done with [unconditional (agape)] love" (1 Cor. 16:14 NKJV).

These firstfruits are out of the righteousness of the Holy Spirit (see Eph. 5:9), which produces a tree of life (see Pro. 11:30) in which this fruit is given to the overcomer to eat, which grows out of the middle of the Paradise of God (see Rev. 2:7). The fruit that you bear is produced through perseverance for those that hear and keep the word of God (see Luk. 8:15) "bearing twelve kinds of fruits, yielding its fruit every month" (Rev. 22:2).

The purpose for bearing the fruit is that the Lord calls us by name as life-bearing Olive trees that are lovely to bear good fruit (see Jer. 11:16). For Jesus says, a "good tree bears good fruit" (Mat. 7:17). The wholesome tongue is what makes you the tree of life (see Pro. 15:4), for it is written, "let no corrupt speech proceed out of your mouth, but only what is good for building others up as the need may be, that it may give grace to those who hear" (Eph. 4:29) for we are to "put off all these: anger, wrath, malice, blasphemy, <u>filthy **language** out of your mouth </u>(Col. 3:8 NKJV underline mine) or any "foolish talking and coarse jesting" (see Eph. 5:4 NKJV) has any inheritance in the Kingdom of God .

For when Generation Zion starts walking in the image of Christ and become a tree of life to the nations, then their leaves become healing for the nations (see Rev. 22:2). These nations are your family, friends, and neighbors. Is this not amazing, my brethren? It certainly is for me. My sisters and brothers in Christ Jesus, are you not excited? I am!

Chapter 13: THE GARMENT OF RAINBOW LIGHT: THE COLOR BLUE

Blue is a primary or main color mentioned in the Tabernacle of Moses that describes an aspect of Jesus as the beloved Son of God (see Luk. 9:35; Rom. 1:4).[33] Blue is widely understood to represent the heavenly realms and the presence of God (the precious Holy Spirit as well), God's throne, God Himself, the Lord's commandments, life (water), healing, and royalty.[34]

THE THREE HEAVENS

We know that there are three heavenly realms, for Paul visited the third heaven (see 2 Cor. 12:2) which are described below:

The first heavenly realm we see is in the natural realm is the blue sky.

The second heavenly realm is where the dominion of the demonic lies "for our wrestling is not against flesh and blood, but against the principalities, against the powers, against the world's rulers of the darkness of this age, and against the spiritual forces of wickedness in the heavenly places" (Eph. 6:12). This is "the intent that now through the assembly the manifold wisdom of God might be made known to the principalities and the powers in the heavenly places" (Eph. 3:10) because it is time to have the hidden things revealed through Christ Jesus, our Lord (see Eph. 3:9, 11).

The second realm is the hidden realm in the first heaven and the second heaven of outer space, which is black. There is no oxygen in outer space, so it kills all life. The enemy is associated with the second heaven because he "comes to steal, kill, and destroy" (John 10:10). The sons of darkness are of the night (see 1 The. 5:5) "the wrath of God is revealed from heaven against all ungodliness and unrighteousness of men who suppress the truth in unrighteousness" (Rom. 1:18).

The third heaven's description is "the expanse that was over their heads was the likeness of a throne, as the appearance of a sapphire stone. On the likeness of the throne was a likeness as the appearance of a man on it above" (Eze. 1:26). The throne of God...in Hebrew...translates to Lapis Lazuli. This semi-precious stone...only comes in blue.[35] The following passages describe the heavenly realm and other depictions of the Bridegroom.

> Moses went up, also Aaron, Nadab, and Abihu, and seventy of the elders of Israel and they saw the God of Israel. And *there was* under His feet as it were a paved work of sapphire stone, and it was like the very heavens in *its* clarity (Exo. 24:9-10 NKJV).

Once the heavenly realm has been activated in you, oh Generation Zion, you start to go up to the roads paved with sapphire stone. That is where you start talking about our Beloved Jesus as more than a king or ruler, but as your intimate affection of life beyond the natural and human emotional bonds of love that manifests "Christ in you the hope of glory" (Col. 1:27). This is where Jesus becomes first in your life; then the revelational transition happens to see Him as "My beloved...His body is like ivory work overlaid with sapphires" (Song 5:10, 14 NKJV).

GOING UP THE SAPPHIRE ROAD

As Generation Zion moves forward in their relationship with the Lord it is a path that is walked on. This path can also be related as the ministry of the feet. It is declared in Isa. 52:7 that it is a ministry to the Body and the lost. It says, "how beautiful on the mountains are the feet of him who brings good news, who publishes peace, who brings good news, who proclaims salvation, who says to Zion, 'Your God reigns!'"

This is the ministry of the evangelist who calls those out of the Babylonian system into the Heavenly realms. The feet ministry is also part of the armor referenced in Eph. 6:15 that the preparation of the Holy Spirit is revealed, and it is declared the enemies of Christ are our footstool (see Heb. 1:13), which signifies the dominion God gave us through Jesus Christ (see Eph. 1:22-23).

As a Body ministry it proclaims peace and good news with encouragement to those that are going through tough times, trials, tribulations, and challenges in their life. When a brother or sister in the Lord is suffering, the person is uplifted in prayer and declaration that no matter the situation "Our God reigns!"

THE SAPPHIRE ROAD LEADS TO MOUNT ZION

The coming prophetic Scripture is "it will happen that the mountain of Yahweh's temple will be established on the top of the mountains, and it will be exalted above the hills; and peoples will stream to it. Many nations will go and say, 'Come! Let's go up to the mountain of Yahweh, and to the house of the God of Jacob; and he will teach us of his ways, and <u>we will walk in his paths</u>.' For the law will go out of Zion, and Yahweh's word from Jerusalem...and I will make that which was lame a remnant, and that which was cast far off a strong nation: and Yahweh will reign over them on Mount Zion from then on, even forever" (Mic. 4:1-2, 7 underline mine).

The path of the Lord is summed up in the law of Christ which is a summary of the ten commandments. Jesus spoke that "you shall love the Lord your God with all your heart, with all your soul, and with all your mind. This is the first and great commandment. A second likewise is this, 'You shall love your neighbor as yourself.' The whole law and the prophets depend on these two commandments." (Mat. 22:37-40). Generation Zion will separate themselves from the things that entangle them to the worldly systems and will naturally walk as forerunners for the King of Glory.

As Generation Zion progresses in their relationship with Christ Jesus they will have the ability to reflect the inlaid heavenly sapphire stone pathway in their lives (see Exo. 24:10). This pathway leads to Mount Zion the dwelling place of God (see Isa. 8:18). As we continue up this pathway, we can bear the image of the heavenly Man (see 1 Cor. 15:49) while the God of peace will crush Satan under our feet shortly (see Rom. 16:20) for "He subdues nations under us, and peoples under our feet" (Psa. 47:3).

This shows that the earthly realm is under our feet, for we sit together in the heavenly places in Christ Jesus (see Eph. 2:5-7). Being under our feet is also a sign of dominion and authority that is only in Christ Jesus where the Father has given the Believer the right to rule (see Mat. 24:45-47).

THE GENERATION ZION NAZARITES

The Generation Zion "Nazirites [or those that separate themselves from the world and consecrate themselves to the Word,] were brighter than snow and whiter than milk; they were more ruddy in body than rubies, *like* sapphire in their appearance" (Lam. 4:7 NKJV brackets mine). Those Nazirites bear the purity of the Word; with brightness, they shine like a diamond intricately formed in Christ Jesus's image. They also know the Word of God inside and out. They can possess the enemy's gates leading and teaching the newborn spiritual babies of Christ, that desire the pure milk of the word (see 1 Pet. 2:2). They are human in physical form, yet the Spirit's nature and appearance come out from the Heavenly realm which lives in them.

These called-out ones burn with passion to the Holy One of Israel because their whole body is immersed in Christ Jesus and "know him, and the power of his resurrection, and the fellowship of his sufferings, becoming conformed to his death" (Phil. 3:10). They deny themselves and daily take up their cross (see Luk. 9:23), while daily, they become more and more conformed to the image and nature God's Son (see Rom. 8:29).

JOINED IN THE HEAVENLY REALMS

Generation Zion operates in joint communion with the Spirit in the heavenly realms of eternal life. This communion is based on the walk of the sapphire stone pathway. There is a correlation between the Hebrew and Greek words that are rendered male and female nouns.

In Hebrew word for Sapphire, is "sap.per," which is masculine. In Greek the word is "sapphiros" and is feminine. The relationship is that the pathway is provided by the Bridegroom God and the Bride walks the pathway He has laid. The Bridegroom God and the Bride work together in unity.

For "what therefore God has joined together, let no man separate" (Mark 10:9) and as being joined to Jesus we are "joint heirs with Christ, if indeed we suffer with him, that we may also be glorified with him" (Rom. 8:17 NKJV).

Being joined together with Jesus it is written that "the holy city, New Jerusalem, coming down out of heaven from God, prepared like a bride adorned for her husband" (Rev. 21:2), which the New Jerusalem is the Bride whose second foundation is sapphire (see Rev. 21:19). The first two foundations of the New Jerusalem represent the complete restoration of the apostles and prophets (see Eph. 2:20; Rev. 21:14) who see and hear in the Heavenly realms. For they have been the most afflicted, restricted, rejected, and misunderstood ministries of the body. Their stones are laid down by the Lord with colorful gems and whose foundations are laid with sapphires (see Isa. 54:11).

Those that bear the image of the heavenly Man see and hear in the prophetic realm to the very heart of the God of Israel. Why? For Generation Zion will see the heavens in clarity due to walking the sapphire stone pathway (see Exo. 24:9-10).

TRANSITION FROM GREEN TO BLUE: DRINKING OF THE HEAVENLY LIVING WATER

In the rainbow garment of light, the color green is manifested and transitioned into the color blue that life and mercy come only from the heavenly realm of the true Mount Zion. Where the river of life flows out of the throne of God for providing living water to those that are thirsty. Jesus wants to encourage Generation Zion with these words:

> "It is done! I am the Alpha and the Omega, the Beginning, and the End. I will give of the fountain of the water of life freely to him who thirsts" (Rev. 21:6 NKJV) "but whoever drinks of the water that I will give him will never thirst again; but the water that I will give him will become in him a well of water springing up to eternal life" (John 4:13-14). "I came that they may have life, and may have it abundantly" (John 10:10).

Because nothing separates us from God's love and life Generation Zion will be able to proclaim with a loving and joyful heart the following Scripture:

> I will greatly rejoice in Yahweh! My soul will be joyful in my God, for he has clothed me with the garments of salvation. He has covered me with the robe of righteousness, as a bridegroom decks himself with a garland and as a bride adorns herself with her jewels (Isa. 61:10).

When in communion with the Father and Son the following happens. The "bridegroom whose voice is of mirth rejoices over his bride, whose voice is of gladness, so your God will rejoice over you" (see Isa. 62:5; Jer. 16:9) through the Holy Spirit, who is 'the testimony of Jesus is the Spirit of Prophecy' (see Rev. 19:10). The Generation Zion Bride with the Holy Spirit announces with fervent "Come!" He who hears, let him say, "Come!" He who is thirsty, let him come. He who desires, let him take the water of life freely" (Rev. 22:17).

Chapter 14: THE GARMENT OF RAINBOW LIGHT: THE COLOR INDIGO

Indigo is made up of blending red/scarlet, blue, and purple colors.[36] Indigo is described in the Levitical priesthood garments and the tabernacle. In the usage in the priesthood garments were in the ephod (Exo. 39:2), breastplate (Exo. 39:8), the pomegranates that are on the hem of the high priest's robe (Exo. 39:24), and the sash (Exo. 39:29). In the usage in the tabernacle God instructed Moses to use indigo in the following way:

> you shall <u>make a veil of blue, and purple, and scarlet, and fine twined linen</u>, with cherubim. It shall be the work of a skillful workman. You shall hang it on four pillars of acacia overlaid with gold; their hooks shall be of gold, on four sockets of silver. You shall hang up the veil under the clasps, and shall bring the ark of the covenant in there within the veil. <u>The veil shall separate the holy place from the most holy</u> for you. You shall put the mercy seat on the ark of the covenant in the most holy place (Exo. 26:31-34 underline mine).

TRANSITION FROM BLUE TO INDIGO

In the rainbow garment of light, the color blue is manifested and transitioned into the color indigo by building bridges between the world of the natural man and the overcoming man. "Don't be overcome by evil, but overcome evil with good" (Rom. 12:21). Jesus wants us to overcome (see Rev. 2-3).

This is the in-between realm of the heavenly throne to rule and reign. You can only rule and reign when you have passed through the blood of Jesus Christ (red/scarlet), manifested the Heavenly realm in speech, conduct in the temporal and the eternal (blue), then transition to the reigning in life that Jesus has predestined you to (purple). It is not just a physical reigning as a king but having your flesh under your feet. "I say, walk by the Spirit, and you won't fulfill the lust of the flesh" (Gal. 5:16) and manifesting the fruit of the Spirit (see Gal. 5:22-23). This is the realm where your belonging "to Christ have crucified the flesh with its passions and lusts" (Gal. 5:24 NKJV).

To get into this realm, you must pass through the veil of the temple that is torn in two from top to bottom (see Mat. 27:51) that leads into the Holy of Holies. That is where God can dwell with you. Once you have entered this realm, there is no veil of limitation. This is the realm where you start manifesting "Christ in you" (Col. 1:27). This realm is where:

> someone turns to the Lord, the veil is taken away. Now the Lord is the Spirit and where the Spirit of the Lord is, there is liberty. But we all, with unveiled face seeing the glory of the Lord as in a mirror, are transformed into the same image from glory to glory, even as from the Lord, the Spirit (2 Cor. 3:16-18).

This is the realm where things are under your feet, and your body comes into the rest of the Lord, which is in you. This indigo realm is where the Heavenly man is starting to manifest. Please know that this is where I believe we can begin to flow in the realm of Christ Jesus, "who is able to do exceedingly abundantly above all that we ask or think, according to the power that works in us" (Eph. 3:20). I call this realm "do you believe?" Do you dare to believe? Generation Zion will you dare yourself to enter in the indigo color of the rainbow garment of light? Are you ready to flow in the finality of Tabernacles or the fulness of the Spirit without measure (see John 3:34)?

Chapter 15: THE GARMENT OF RAINBOW LIGHT: THE COLOR PURPLE

The color of purple was rare, and only the elite or the rich possessed it. It is associated with royalty, for only those of royal or nobility could obtain it during Biblical times. It is a primary color mentioned in the Tabernacle of Moses. This final color in the rainbow garment of light is the realm of no limitations.

REIGNING IN PURPLE

Purple is defined in Scripture as it is seen and associated with royalty according to the book of Judges. Judges 8:26 describes that "purple robes...*were* on the kings of Midian." Please note that I am only associating this Scripture and all the remaining Scriptures that describe purple was costly and associated with wealthy people.

The wealth and power of the color purple is seen through the following Scriptures showing that those in the Babylonian system may for a time be clothed with false clothing of "fine linen, purple, and scarlet, and decked with gold and precious stones and pearls" (see Rev. 18:16) or false power and wealth which represents the Babylonian satanic/demonic kingdom, not God's kingdom.

In Luke 16:19-31, the words of Jesus tell us of a certain rich man that was clothed in "purple and fine linen" who ended up in Hades because of unbelief in God's Word.

Daniel 5:29 tells that Daniel was "clothed...with purple and put a chain of gold around his neck and made a proclamation concerning him that he should be the third ruler in the kingdom."

Anyone in the Babylonian system rejects God and His sovereignty and His Son in whom He sent (see Luk. 10:16). When you come to Jesus Christ, you have forsaken the Babylonian or worldly/sophisticated system of wealth and power. You are no longer a child of the world but have been "delivered us out of the power of darkness, and translated us into the Kingdom of the Son of his love" (Col. 1:13 NKJV).

Daniel represents the Bride of Christ clothed with royalty (see 1 Pet. 2:9) and as the third ruler, meaning we are "kings and priests to our God; and we will reign on the earth" (see Rev. 5:10). According to the seventh angel's voice and multiple voices in Heaven declaring, "The kingdom of the world has become the Kingdom of our Lord, and of his Christ. He will reign forever and ever" (Rev. 11:15). This is for all Overcomers of Generation Zion who is the Bride who are known as His anointed ones on Earth. They are the mouthpieces or oracles to the Body and this Earth. They write and speak the mysteries of Heaven with power.

TRANSITION FROM INDIGO TO PURPLE: THE REALM OF NO LIMITATIONS

In the rainbow garment of light, the color of indigo is manifested and transitioned into the color purple, the final color of the rainbow, you have come into the realm of no limitations. These men and women are "led by the Spirit of God, these are children of God" (Rom. 8:14), in which "the creation waits with eager expectation for the children of God to be revealed" (Rom. 8:19).

When Generation Zion walks in this realm of life they are in God's presence where we may participate in the true wealth of God. This wealth is where we are united and are an abiding place for Him. We truly manifest "I in Him and Him in me" (see John 17:21, 23) where we walk in the full stature representing our commission as royal Melchizedek *Šô ʿēr (Sho-Air)* or Thoo-ror-ros warrior priestly kings. This realm of no limitations is where Generation Zion participates in

His mighty power that is really for the age to come (see Heb. 6:5) now.[37]

This is the realm where the miraculous happens. Generation Zion will be able to command the winds to be still (see Mark 4:39); handkerchiefs or aprons are being used from your body to heal sickness and disease, and the evil spirits leave people (see Acts 19:12). This is the realm of the Spirit without measure (see John 3:34). This is where the dead are physically raised to life, the blind eyes are seen, the unconventional becomes conventional, arms; and fingers grow out, other recreative miracles happen, leprosy or gross skin diseases are cleansed, the Heavenly wisdom operates at its fullness, etc. Why does this happen? Because at this level, you are a tree of life that operates with the leaves of healing (see Rev. 22:2). Your nature is so submitted to the Holy Spirt that like Jesus, "you are willing" (see Mat. 8:3; Mark 1:41; Luk. 5:13 NKJV).

Part III – THE WARFARE OF "AGAPAO" (UNCONDITIONAL LOVE IN ACTION)

Chapter 16: FIGHTING FROM A SEATED POSITION

Generation Zion while wearing the rainbow garment of light can do nothing by themselves, yet they co-labor in warfare with Christ Jesus in them. Whether the war is "guerilla" or jungle or land or desert or sea, the warfare is to be seen and done in the cosmic arrays of spiritual life blending into the natural ways of humanity.

When wearing the rainbow garment and prior to going to battle you must "gird up your loins" (see 1 Kin. 18:46 NKJV). Peter writes that when we are to "gird up our loins" it is the loins of our mind (see 1 Pet. 1:13 NKJV). For the enemies plans are to distract the thought processes, patterns, and plans prior, during, and after entering spiritual warfare.

GIRD UP YOUR LOINS

The Old Testament warriors would wear this garment or tunic with a belt or called a girdle around it. Mobility is necessary when fighting. When the garment is fluid around your body you are unable to fight. Each "Šô'ēr"/"Thoo-ro-ros" must take their garment/tunic and do the following to fight. Spiritually hoist it up above the knees, wrap it around your backside, bring the material between your legs, take the extra material and tie it around your front.[38] Now we gird up our mental and spiritual loins by taking our thoughts captive.

Our Position in Agape Love to Fight the Enemy

There are 24 *Šô'ēr* (Sho-Air)/ Throo-ros-ros (Gatekeepers) garments, to be discussed in other books, that are put on us that we position ourselves to do warfare "against the principalities, against the powers, against the world's rulers of the darkness of this age, and against the spiritual forces of wickedness in the heavenly places" (Eph. 6:12). Below is a list of the garments used by the Generation Zion warrior priest kings. They are used in the preparation and conjunction with the rainbow garment of light in spiritual warfare. Most of the garments are to be elaborated on in upcoming publications. They are:

1. The Garment of Rainbow Light (discussed in Part II).

2. The Garment of Salvation.

3. Clothed in Scarlet.

4. The Garment of Salvation/<u>Deliverance</u>.

5. The Garment of Praise.

6. Clothed with Gladness.

7. Clothed with Righteousness.

8. Clothed with Pure Bright Linen and White Robes and Palm Branches in Hands.

9. Raiment of Needlework.

10. Clothing of Gold.

11. Clothed and Girded with Strength

12. Clothed with a Cloud.

13. Clothed with Our Heavenly Habitation.

14. Apparel of Red.

15. The Garments of Vengeance.

16. Chests Wrapped with Golden Sashes.

17. Clothed with Purple.

18. Clothed with "Hode" and "Haw-dawr'" or Splendor and Majesty/Honor.

19. The Fine Linen Ephod Robe.

20. Robe of Righteousness.

21. Robe of Justice.

22. Clothed with Humility.

23. Turban of Justice

24. The Crown of Holiness.

I want to reiterate that when we warfare that we are to remember Paul's words:

For though we walk in the flesh, we don't wage war according to the flesh; for the weapons of our warfare are not of the flesh, but mighty before God to the throwing down of strongholds, throwing down imaginations and every high thing that is exalted against the knowledge of God and bringing every thought into captivity to the obedience of Christ (2 Cor. 10:3-5 NKJV).

THE ROYAL PRAYER CLOTH

The Jewish people when they prayed in the temple wore an outer garment that is a prayer cloth. The prayer cloth, though separate from the garment of rainbow light is the covering that every Jewish male wore from the age of 13 after their bar-mitzvah. The Lord directed the Israelites to make the tassels. "You shall make tassels on the four corners of the clothing with which you cover yourself" (Deut. 22:12 NKJV). The prayer cloth that Jesus wore is mentioned as a garment. When the woman with the issue of blood touched Jesus's garment (see Mat. 9:20-22), it was his prayer shawl. And as many as touched it were made perfectly well (see Mat. 14:36). "Wherever he entered, into villages, or into cities, or into the country, they laid the sick in the marketplaces, and begged him that they might just touch the fringe/tassel of his garment; and as many as touched him were made well" (Mark 6:56). In our true Heavenly culture, it is called a tallit and tzitzit it was considered "'innerwear' *tallit* with only the fringes visible (tzitzit). Rich Robinson writes in the article *The Tallit and Tzitzit*:

> Originally the *tallit* was a four-cornered outer garment to which were attached the fringes, or *tzitzit*...The real significance of the *tallit* is not in the garment itself, but in the fringes... The *tzitzit* (tassels), however, are."[39]

This is where the tassels of the heart are joined to the *tzitzit*. A blue cord is woven into the *tzitzit* or prayer cloth.
Rich Robinson continues in *The Tallit and Tzitzit*:

> In ancient times, tassels were part of the hem of a garment, and the hem symbolized the wearer's authority... it was also used with the curtains of the tabernacle where God dwelt "enthroned" between the cherubim (see 1 Sam. 4:4; Isa. 37:16) ...They spoke of royalty and kingship. Even today we talk of "royal blue" and "royal purple" from the custom of Roman emperors who wore purple mantles...Jesus's garment

had tassels at the hem and "the tassels added to the hem were not worn by commoners, but by the nobility or royalty."[40]

Thank you, Jesus, that we are a royal priesthood. Reinaugurated after the ascension of Jesus Christ.

THE TASSELS OF THE HEART

As God reigns in the life of Generation Zion the Holy Spirit is encouraging them to use the analogy of the four tassels of the prayer cloth and apply it to the four areas of their hearts. He proclaims:

> "My children, I have made tassels on the corners of the garments of your heart. I have put a blue thread in the corner tassels. You shall have those tassels tied to you for the purpose of remembering all the commandments of God, the law of Christ, and do them" ... "and be holy for your God" (see Num. 15:38-40; Gal. 6:2).

> The law of Christ is summed up by Jesus as "you shall love the Lord your God with all your heart, with all your soul, and with all your mind.'This is the first and great commandment. A second likewise is this, 'You shall love your neighbor as yourself.'The whole law and the prophets depend on these two commandments" (Mat. 22:37-40).

Those tassels are made up of "a threefold cord [that] is not quickly broken" (Ecc. 4:12 brackets mine). This means that each Christian, the Holy Spirit, and the third heavenly cord of Christ's law is not quickly broken for "says Yahweh, "and I am God. Yes, since the day was, I am he. There is no one who can deliver out of my hand. I will work, and who can hinder it?'" (Isa. 43:12-13).

The Lord Jesus reminds us that "My sheep hear my voice, and I know them, and they follow me.I give eternal life to them. They will never perish, and no one will snatch them out of my hand. My Father who has given them to me is greater than all. No one is able to snatch them out of my Father's hand" (John 10:27-29).

These tassels cannot be broken easily because they are in Jesus's hand, and the Father's hand is wrapped around Jesus's, showing double authority and blessing. "For I am persuaded that neither death, nor life, nor angels, nor principalities, nor things present, nor things to come, nor powers, nor height, nor depth, nor any other created thing will be able to separate us from God's love which is in Christ Jesus our Lord" (Rom. 8:38-39).

As the tassels that are tied to the prayer shall represent communion with God and prayer to fight the good fight. When it is pulled over your face you are in a private holy of holies.

When you pray the Holy Spirit becomes your spiritual prayer shall. I am not saying to go get one, but if you have one, use it. For out of prayer comes the light of life that binds you to God. For Jesus says, "It is the Spirit that gives life. The flesh ·doesn't give life [^L is useless; counts for nothing]. The words I told you ·are spirit, and they give life [*or* are from the Spirit who gives life]" (John 6:63 The Expanded Bible (EXB)). Pray the Scriptures, sing the Scriptures, live the Scriptures.

A SEATED POSITION OF WARFARE

Peter wrote that you are to "gird up the loins of your mind" (1 Pet. 1:13 NKJV) in addition your heart must be prepared for war. This is accomplished by having your attitude in alignment with the Father's will and that you know your position of authority. The fight is in the Spirit realm which is taken from the position of being seated in the heavenlies. For it is written that God has "made us to sit with him in the heavenly places in Christ Jesus" (Eph. 2:6). We are then made "holy and without defect and blameless before him" (Col. 1:22) because God "chose us in him before the foundation of the world, that we would be holy and without defect before him in [agape or perfect unconditional] love" (Eph. 1:4).

This declaration of war is taken from a victorious point of view. There are strategies that the Holy Spirit will give us. Obedience is necessary for total defeat. The defeat and destruction that we fight with comes from the knowledge that we are royal ambassadors for the Messiah and our Heavenly Father (see 2 Cor. 5:20).

As we fight, we know that "He [Jesus] lets us rule as kings and serve God His Father as priests" (Rev. 1:6 (CEV)). When a king makes a decree, it usually comes from a seated position on his throne. Paul tells us our heavenly position is from an established seated view. It is a term of authority that only the king can revoke once it is proclaimed.

When fighting in the Spirit realm with the strategies provided, it flows directly from the thrones of God the Father and God the Son. We positionally stand-in is the knowledge that we are kings and that we flow under the unction of the Holy Spirit's anointing to function.

The Holy Spirit's power is a mighty river with rapids from two different streams. One stream is of oil, and the other stream is water. The sons of Korah wrote, "there is a river, the streams of which make the city of God glad, the holy place of the tents of the Most High" (Psa. 46:4).

The Holy Spirit gives us the proper stream to flow in depending on the need. Depending on which stream of the Spirit's power is being used it will always rejuvenate by washing over you with refreshment. We know that the Holy Spirit's power is directed from the thrones of the Father and the Son.

THE WEAPONS OF OFFENSIVE PRAYER

We have multiple offensive weapons that we are given to fight with. The knowledge of these weapons is shared between the Old and New Testaments. The most notable of the offensive weapons is the Sword of the Spirit.

The garment of praise, which uses many forms and weapons, is used with the musicians (praise/worship) and/or prayer warriors that go forth into battle first. We are to "pray at all times in the Spirit with every prayer and request, and stay alert in this with all perseverance and intercession for all the saints" (Eph. 6:18 Holmon Christian Standard Bible (HCSB)). Generation Zion must be in an attitude of constant prayer and trusting God at every moment that "whatever you do, in word or in deed, do all in the name of the Lord Jesus, giving thanks to God the Father, through him" (Col. 3:17). It is not easy living the Christian life. It is not fun a lot of times when it is contrary to the natural principles of the mind. But it is rewarding at the end of the day. Without prayer, it is like having the receiver of a wired telephone off the hook. When you pray, your communication with God is always on. With that in mind, we are to "stay alert and be persistent in your prayers for all believers everywhere" (Eph. 6:18b NLT). Prayer is the oxygen needed to survive life's trials and tribulations. **When we feel the least like praying, that is when we need to pray the most.**

We must constantly be in prayer because we are constantly in danger. When we have neglected our prayer life, that is when the enemy attacks the most. This is when he takes advantage of us the most. When we are in prayer, we are in the safety of God's arms and wrapped in His presence.

Satan's Schemes to Thwart God's Presence

David Jeremiah describes the enemy's plans to thwart us from living in God's presence by discouraging us in a depressive attitude. Satan and his cohorts will do anything that derails us from having an active dialogue of listening and speaking with the Holy Spirit.[41]

It is within the council of God that you receive His counsel for the assignments He wants you to fulfill. David Jeremiah goes onto to comment that through doubt, denial, and deception Satan will impede the counsel and integrity of God's instructions and purpose in our lives to thwart his plans in *Spiritual Warfare Terms of Engagement Study Guide.*[42]

Are you willing to stand by the Scriptures that define our Melchizedekian warrior priesthood positions as having royal power? Remember, it is not by any control or influence of our own but Him that lives in you. "God's Spirit is in you and is more powerful than the one that is in the world" (1 John 4:4b CEV). We understand that as children of God, we go in Jesus's name with His authority and blessing to wage war. But you must make sure you have the training before the time of proper warfare.

MESSAGE FROM THE FATHER AND SON

The Holy Spirit is saying to us:

"Beloved, Generation Zion train, train, train, practice, do not goad the devil, for he is cunning, crafty, and deceiving. Do not be fooled by the mixing of unclean and strange fire. This fire is mixed with false religion that goes against the knowledge of My Son, Jesus Christ. I want the best for you.

"The training is knowing My Son's voice. The training is based on learning Our Words, written (logos) and prophetic (rhema) that live in you. Stand upon My promises that I have written on paper to renew your minds and hearts. My Word brings physical, emotional, and spiritual healing.

"I love [agapao] you more than you can imagine. Stay holy and pure in My ways. Do not give in to false teachings that pervert My Word. It is through the Cross that leads to Me and the blood of My Son.

"As you stand, be conformed to the weapons of My battle-ax, My bow and arrows, My spear, the lightning power that is sustained and executed from My hands. It is by My Spirit that this power and authority is given. My greatest training strategy is to flow from Me and My Father's heart and My mind through prayer, fasting, and worshiping of Me (Jesus).

"Do not always look to engage the enemy. Though he is great, I am greater. Be led by My Spirit to engage the enemy. To possess and gain the ground I have given you. You must be prayed up and know My voice."

Chapter 17: THE MULTI-DIRECTIONAL DIMENSION OF PRAYER

It takes faith that your prayers are answered by believing in the One who answers them. As believers in the Generation Zion army, we are called first and foremost to help and pray for our brothers and sisters in Christ so that the Holy Spirit can use them to their fullest potential.

THE INTERCESSORY PRAYERS OF FAITH

David Jeremiah in *Spiritual Warfare Terms of Engagement Study Guide* discusses the following principles about intercession and the shield of faith.

Intercession is a principle that has a purpose calling to pray for other saints. The person praying is an intercessor. When the focus of praying for others, our problems seem to become less serious. [44]

Christians working together are a community made up of individuals that are protected in prayer by faith in the Lord Jesus Christ. It is by this faith that we are joined in the defense of one another. [45]

Stu Weber writes in *Spirit Warriors* that this community of faith protects each other utilizing the shield of faith with interlocked shields. This family that you join is a group of soldiers that are needed to march with. They can be members of a church, a Facebook prayer group, or just an accountability partner that become units of faith. [46]

The Returned Lightning Prayers

In *The Lost Art of Intercession* written by Jim W. Goll gives an in-depth teaching of multi-directional praying. Multi-directions prayers are first received upward and then reciprocated downward. It is through

intercessors and intercession that these prayers and praises as sweet-smelling aromas to our Father are sent to His throne. and received in confidence back to us with signs and wonders.[47]
In Scripture according to the epistle of the Revelation of Jesus Christ chapter 8 gives a vivid description of how multi-directional prayers work.

> Another angel came and stood at the altar, holding a golden censer; and much incense was given to him, so that he might [a1]add it to the prayers of all the [b2]saints on the golden altar which was before the throne.And the smoke of the incense ascended from the angel's hand with the prayers of the [c3]saints before God. Then the angel took the censer and filled it with the fire of the altar, and hurled it to the earth; and there were peals of thunder and sounds, and flashes of lightning and an earthquake (Rev. 8:3-5 NASB).

As Generation Zion Melchizedek royal priests' job is to restore the fire from His presence using intercessors to bring an altar of sweet-smelling incense of aromatic prayers where the fire of God is blazing hot to the needy ones.[48] From the above passage in Revelation among the many "wonders" is lightning that plummets "downward" from the hands of God to strike the mark of returned prayer which displays His presence.[49]

---

1. https://www.biblegateway.com/ passage/?search=Rev.+8%3A3-5+&version=NASB#fen-NASB-30819a

2. https://www.biblegateway.com/ passage/?search=Rev.+8%3A3-5+&version=NASB#fen-NASB-30819b

3. https://www.biblegateway.com/ passage/?search=Rev.+8%3A3-5+&version=NASB#fen-NASB-30820c

Job makes a wonderful description of God's lighting that strikes the mark and declares His presence that goes forth to all the Earth's ends.

> He covers *His* hands with the lightning, and commands it to strike the mark. Its noise declares His presence...at this also my heart trembles, and leaps from its place. Listen closely to the thunder of His voice, and the rumbling that goes out from His mouth. Under the whole heaven He lets it loose, and His lightning to the ends of the earth (Job 36:32-37:3 NASB1995).

When the prayers of Generation Zion who are wrapped in the rainbow garment of light are lifted "up" to the Father's throne through intercession releases anointed lighting prayers of God's Word to intercede for the situation. The return answers are heralded "down" displaying God's judgment in striking down the enemies of the situation and accomplishing through faith the Father's command.[50]

Answered Prayers Bring God's Presence and Angels

As we continue to intercede daily for people, praying and worshiping Him, He may choose to visit us physically. This happens when His child comes to Him with a heart that is controlled by pure love, contriteness, purity, and the person wants to draw close to their Heavenly Father.

For God says, "then you will call upon Me and go and pray to Me, and I will listen to you. And you will seek Me and find *Me,* when you search for Me with all your heart.I will be found by you, says the Lord" (Jer. 29:12-14a NKJV). James also reiterates that as you "draw near to God, and he will draw near to you" (Jam. 4:8a). With those prayers going up to Him, He sends His lightning down to us. When that lightning hits the ground, it produces smoke of His "manifest presence" or "glory cloud."

As His presence shows up, the angels come with Him. Gabriel declares to Mary that he stands in the presence of God (see Luk. 1:19). Some seraphim encircle the throne of God (see Isa. 6:1-2a). The cherubim also are in the presence of God, for they are embroidered in the curtains to the Holy of Holies (see Exo. 26:1; Exo. 36:35). They are built onto the mercy seat of God (see Exo. 37:7-9; Heb. 9:5), they are carved on the doors of Ezekiel's temple (Eze. 41:25).

TWO PROPHETIC PRAYERS FOR GENERATION ZION

PRAYER NO. 1: A PRAYER OF CONTINUAL SACRIFICE

Pray the following prayer from *The Lost Art of Intercession* by Jim W. Goll for continual sacrifice Generation Zion:

> Let's offer up the continual sacrifice of praise and the incense of prayer. And let us continue to do so until the angels take their censer, fill it to the brim, and cast Heaven's *fire on the altar* back down to into our earthly dwelling places again.[51]

PRAYER NO. 2: A PRAYER AGAINST SPIRITUAL SUICIDE

How many times is discouragement battled? The enemy plans to kill you spiritually, allowing us to give up and have spiritual suicide. I want pray this prayer with you:

> Unholy, wicked, and evil serpent spirit of suicide in the name of Jesus, whose name is greater in authority, power, and in every other way and form imaginable than yours, I command you to release your nasty grip off my brothers and sisters that read this. In Jesus' name, you are to unwrap, untangle, and uncoil yourself from their minds, hearts, and emotions.
>
> Any holes where your poisonous and toxic venom has struck and hardened into thoughts of the grave, I pluck them out and, with the water of the Holy Spirit, drain and clean the

corrosion of negative thoughts toward themselves. I call upon the blood of Jesus, where He took 39 innocent stripes for your healing to fill and seal those holes emotionally and physically.

In the name of Jesus, I use the Sword of the Spirit or the rhomphaia that proceeds from the mouth of Jesus according to Rev. 2:16 to cut the head of the serpent spirit of spiritual suicide off your life. Let its head and body stop withering and come into subjection under our feet with no backlash, retaliation, retribution, revenge, and destruction of wrapping itself against us or snapping us back with its fangs. Let it go under our feet where its master and father are in the mighty name of Jesus. Amen.

Chapter 18: THE CO-LABORING SUNG PRAYERS OF SAINTS AND ANGELS

Throughout the Scriptures, angels have been involved in Supernatural wonders. Our relationship with them in praise and worship, warfare, and judgments are unique.

THE FIVE PREMISES OF WORKING WITH ANGELS

1. Through intercession we co-labor by releasing angelic visitations.
2. The destiny of individuals and nations are determined through intercession.
3. An innumerable number of angels are awaiting to be assigned and released.
4. The involvement of angels in all facets of daily life is the result of prayer.
5. Answered prayers are often provided by angels.[52]

The Sung Prayers of Intercession and Entreatment

With an innumerable number of angels, we get to sing to the God of eternal love. Like our Hebrew family, whose prayers go back thousands of years, and angels who go back before the creation of planet Earth we have the pleasure and honor to sing prayers to our living God. It is also worth noting that the eternal loving God receives the sung prayers with great anticipation.

In English, the word "prayer" is translated from the Hebrew word "tephillah." The meaning of this word is used for "intercession, supplication; by implication, a hymn: —prayer."[53] The term occurs in 70 verses 77 times. In the Genesius' Hebrew-Chaldee Lexicon, this word is used in three definitions: "intercession, deprecation, entreaty, supplication, prayer, hymn, or sacred song." Psalms 1-72 and Habakkuk 3:1 is described in English as prayers but are sung prayers.[54]

Jim W. Goll, in *The Lost Art of Intercession* defines a usage of *tephillah* as intercessory prayers of judgments of God in reference to Psalms 1-72. The high priest would join in through his ministry of prayer and praise.[55] God listens to the prayers of the saints with fervent intercession before releasing any type of judgment for the purposes of establishing mercy and ending judgment.[56]

THE BRIDAL PRAYERS

Tephillah is commonly translated in Greek as "pros-yoo-khay."[57] What is interesting to note is that they are both feminine nouns in Hebrew and Greek. Another meaning to this is that they are sung prayers sent from the Bride's Bridal chamber to her Bridegroom (Jesus Christ). The Bridal Chamber is in the recesses of the heart of each person in Generation "ZION."

These songs are more than ordinary songs or prayers. They are songs or prayers conveyed from the Bride's heart. They are the heart-rendering or lovesick songs of a person in love with their Bridegroom. The Bridal prayers include the pleasures that the Holy Spirit provides in joy and peace when a wife knows her husband will protect her in the hour of need. Rejoice and know that Jesus Christ is here to protect you in your hour of need and any other time.

In Isaiah 56, when prophetically speaking of the Gentiles becoming part of the Household of God, in verse 7 when speaking, God calls His "house of prayer" a *house of tephillah* or house of sung prayer. Music is so integral. This statement shows that when we congregate and sing our petitions to God, He hears us collectively. The following nine Biblical examples are provided in showing us how the Holy Spirit uses are sung (tephillah/pros-yoo-khay) prayers:

1. When Daniel was interceding to the Lord on behalf of his people, his prayers were tephillah (see Dan. 9:17).
2. When Jonah died in the belly of the whale, his prayer was a tephillah that went unto the Lord's holy temple.
3. The prayer or tephillah of Habakkuk about the deliverance and victory of God delivering His people (see Hab. 3:1). This was set to music because, in Hab. 3:19, this tephillah was given to the "music director, on my stringed instruments."
4. Then the priests, the Levites, arose and blessed the people, and their voice was heard; and their prayer (tephillah) came *up* to His holy dwelling place, to heaven (see 2 Chr. 30:27). Something interesting to note is that though there were multiple priests, they were in unity and because it was a single voice, the tephillah went to the Holy dwelling in heaven of God. When people pray in unity in various ways, the Holy Spirit will look down and want to congregate with them.
5. Jesus called His house of prayer a house of "tephillah/pros-yoo-khay" (see Luk. 19:46).
6. When Jesus was praying in the Garden of Gethsemane, His prayers were "pros-yoo-khay/tephillah." He was singing His distresses to His Father.
7. After Jesus ascended back to the Father, it was in the upper room that they were in unity and praying or "tephillah/pros-yoo-khay." At the same time, Judas's replacement had been made, and the baptism of the Holy Spirit of fire had come during the feast of Pentecost (see Act 1:12-2:4).
8. When Peter was set free by an angel, it was with the petition of "tephillah/pros-yoo-khay" or sung prayers without ceasing until this was completed (see Act 12:5-16).

9. The prayers that are being offered up to God are "tephillah/ pros-yoo-khay" (sung prayers) where they are placed in the censer as the incense is filled with the fire of the altar and sent back to Earth where there are voices and thunderings, and flashes of lightning (see Rev. 8:3-4).

The Watchman Prayers

In Ephesians 6:18 (NKJV), we are admonished to be "praying always with all prayer (tephillah/pros-yoo-khay) and supplication in the Spirit, being watchful to this end with all perseverance and supplication for all the saints." By doing this we are instructed to "continue steadfastly in prayer (tephillah/pros-yoo-khay), watching in it with thanksgiving" (Col. 4:2). Then Peter writes, "but the end of all things is near. Therefore be of sound mind, self-controlled, and sober in prayer (tephillah/pros-yoo-khay" (1 Pet. 4:7). A watchman is to know the times and seasons through prayer and fasting with petition made with melody from his heart.

Worshipping PRAYERS

In the Greek language, the act of praying is "pros-yoo'-khom-ahee" which is "to pray to God, i.e., supplicate, worship: — pray."[58] How often have you gone into deep intercession that you receive a melody in your heart, and you start to sing it? This is part of the travail, but it was also a common Hebrew practice. When visiting different Messianic congregations, most prayers have a melodic tune to them. Especially when reading the Scriptures. Do you sing the Scriptures to the Holy Spirit when reading? If you have not. Try it. See if you get a different result.

"When he [Jesus] was praying (pros-yoo'-khom-ahee) in a certain place, one of his disciples said to him, 'Lord, teach us to pray (pros-yoo'-khom-ahee), just as John also taught his disciples.' He said to them, 'when you pray (pros-yoo'-khom-ahee), say'" (Luk. 11:1-2). There is a key to this that Jesus modeled in his prayers of worship that

He inaugurated. The teaching of the word "say" can be used in context to "tell or call upon."[59]

Let us think about it in this context when we pray that we call out to our Heavenly Father in a melody. We do not have to be vain about it but loving toward Him. Out of our hearts, we pour forth our petitions to Him. Generation Zion sing your way to the throne.

Making Melody in Our Hearts

Paul taught a concept of singing that is in Ephesians where we are to be "filled with the Spirit, speaking to one another in psalms, hymns, and spiritual songs; singing and making melody in your heart to the Lord; giving thanks always concerning all things in the name of our Lord Jesus Christ, to God, even the Father" (Eph. 5:18-20).

We are also to "let the word of Christ dwell in you richly; in all wisdom teaching and admonishing one another with psalms, hymns, and spiritual songs, singing with grace in your heart to the Lord" (Col. 3:16).

When the human spirit is continuing to be filled with the Holy Spirit, the melodies pour out of the heart and come forth. Whether they are in an earthly or heavenly language, it does not matter, except that your love for God overflows in a melody of the heart. Where your heart is, there your treasure will be that has been stored up (see Mat. 6:21; Luk. 12:34). The more Word you store in your heart, the more you seek Him. Out of your heart will flow living streams of water that bring forth life to you and those around you (see John 7:38).

Singing Conquers Fear

As we are filled with the Holy Spirit, we are then instructed that His words come out of us because the teachings, wisdom, and building up/admonishing of each other are sung forth. Remember, "there is no fear in love; but perfect love casts out fear, because fear involves torment. But he who fears has not been made perfect in love" (1 John 4:18 NKJV).

"For God has not given us a spirit of fear, but of power and of love and of a sound mind" (2 Tim. 1:7 NKJV). I want you to understand that fear is not love but a tormenting spirit that was not created by God. But it is through love that spirit of fear is broken off you through the deliverance of the mind. The more you build yourself up through prayer and worship, the more you will be able to say "yes, Lord" instead of "why me, Lord?"

When you listen to songs that build you up according to His standards, "He will calm you in his love. He will rejoice over you with singing" (Zeph. 3:17b). The quietness brings peace to your heart. This peace builds confidence so that you can march forward in victory. Every battle God is in, He wins. There is no debating that. He just does.

I want to encourage you with Paul's words:

> who shall separate us from the love of Christ? Could oppression, or anguish, or persecution, or famine, or nakedness, or peril, or sword?... For I am persuaded that neither death, nor life, nor angels, nor principalities, nor things present, nor things to come, nor powers,nor height, nor depth, nor any other created thing will be able to separate us from God's love which is in Christ Jesus our Lord (Rom. 8:35, 38-39).

Be of good cheer that nothing can separate us from God's love which we are given in Christ Jesus our Lord. If you read this and deal with Earthly or natural things that may cause some form of uncomfortableness, they will not be able to separate you from God's love. Why should it? We are His, beloved Generation Zion and once we are in Jesus's hands, nothing can snatch us out of them because they are in the Father's hand too (see John 10:28-29).

Be Strong and Courageous with no fear

God spoke to us about trusting in Him. When we trust Him, we know that there is nothing to fear. Because whether we live or die in the natural world, we will live in the eternal. To start to live in the eternal realm of life on the day that we ask Jesus to live in our hearts. The growth process of trusting is a day-by-day, moment-by-moment process. Below are some Biblical examples of trust:

- God spoke to Abram about the promise of descendants (see Gen. 15:1). Abram had no physical heir. He was an old man past the time of natural usage to procreate, yet he was given a son of promise. This is our spiritual ancestor. When the eternal covenant with God was made, his name was changed from Abram to Abraham. When God came upon Him, He said, "do not be afraid, Abram. I am your shield, your exceedingly great reward" (Gen. 15:1). This is one of the first times that we are encouraged that God is our defender and not to be afraid.

- In 2 Chronicles 32:7-8, it is written:

"Be strong and courageous. Don't be afraid or dismayed because of the king of Assyria, nor for all the multitude who is with him; for there is a greater one with us than with him. An arm of flesh is with him, but Yahweh our God is with us to help us and to fight our battles." The people rested themselves on the words of Hezekiah king of Judah.

This verse mentions that we are also surrounded by a great heavenly host that we cannot see against the king of Assyria or known as the devil. It is with the blood of Jesus that we can conquer our enemies. The victory is in the name of Jesus. The power that conquered the grave put his enemies under His feet. This promise is a current and a future promise. We know that in the Spirit, we have conquered the enemy, but to make it a reality, we must walk through the process of conquering through the power of the Holy Spirit, not by our own strength.

- In Isaiah 41:10, God says, "do not fear, for I am with you, do not be afraid, for I am your God; I will strengthen you, I will help you, I will uphold you with my victorious right hand" (New Revised Standard Version, Updated Edition (NRSVUE)).

This powerful statement declares that when times are tough, the Holy Spirit will strengthen, help, uphold or lift you up because He is victorious. The victory is His, and we gain the benefits. Remember, when something seems huge and unbearable, He is with us bearing it. I encourage you to face it and know that as Jesus is on the throne, it will be ok. But when He comes, all will be made right, and the voice of the wicked will be put in place.

- The Angel of the Lord encourages Joshua to "be strong and courageous…be strong and very courageous" (Jos. 1:6-7). This is the encouragement that when we are afraid, He has our back. How many times will it take for us to learn that? It is not instantaneous. It is a process that is learned. Keep learning.

Walking in Love and Courage

We are encouraged to "consider one another in order to stir up love and good works" (Heb. 10:24 NKJV). When we are no longer walking in fear or discouragement, we can then help our brothers or sisters with the ability to provoke them to love another, which produces good works. By our faith in Jesus, we walk in "agapao" love, which will produce fruit. This fruit is done by working at it. Do you work and cultivate the fruit that is growing from your branches?

These branches need to produce fruit. The fruit is grown by walking about in God's love towards humanity and representing Jesus to the world. This is what He commands that we represent His love by loving each other. This peculiar love or "agapao" (unconditional love in action) is given, which produces the light of God in us. It is God's light that brings those trapped in darkness out. The light must be turned on for darkness to flee.

In Ephesians 5:2a, we are admonished to "walk in love, even as Christ also loved us." Generation Zion when Christ's love is enveloped in your heart you will think like Him. His love transcends emotions and intellect. What I mean is that when we see things from the point of view of righteousness, we can know that emotions can lead us astray. Healthy love is built on the love of Jesus, who died in our place. This is the sacrificial love we are to have for each other.

That does not mean to be a scapegoat. Yet are you willing to stick your neck out for God's truth and bring truth to your friend who is in error? If that person has done something wrong, will you stir up their love for God's righteousness in their lives? Will you help them admit their wrongs and get in right standing with God and recompense their wrongs?

When we walk in love and courage, we do not give up assembling, but we encourage one another to walk in the light, bear good fruit, love each other, do not give up, teach the love of the Lord through the Cross that brings us back to right standing with God. This is love. Why? Because we know that the time of God's judgments has begun and that we must be prepared.

RENEW LIKE AN EAGLE

Like an eagle, we are encouraged to go through the process of growing in God's love and shed off the corruption in our life according to Isaiah 40:31:

> But those who wait for Yahweh will renew their strength.
> They will mount up with wings like eagles.
> They will run, and not be weary.
> They will walk, and not faint.

As we study this passage, it shows that while waiting, there is a process of growth during a season of refreshment. We will be refreshed by renewal. That means to be new again. It is a point of view that when we get old and worn out, we take, as you would say, rest; we become new again. We become young, as you would say. Able to endure more.

During the renewal process, we gain the strength that helps us fly up spiritually into the heavenly places. These are greater realms of love that act within "agapao" to display the calling of God in your life. These heavenly places will help you run the race to the next elevational height of glory. It is not just another level of promotion but a deeper understanding of the foundation of Christ in your life.

These ariel views seen are the prophetic mantles of grace, mercy, love, encouragement, peace, and longsuffering. When you walk through these processes in the Lord Jesus Christ, you will not get weary or weak, nor will you faint from exhaustion. The Holy Spirit helps you through this so you can help others. That is why when you are being hidden in God; it is for the time of restoration, which encompasses your renewal. When you have been renewed, you see a revolution of past behaviors that are not of a Godly kingdom mentality get stripped away. For revival happens first within your heart, then anyone else God places in your life to help revive.

CONCLUSION

Generation Zion arise and take hold of what the Holy Spirit has been waiting for over two thousand years. We are in a time where things are upside down and what is defined as right is wrong, good as evil, Godly and ungodly are reversed.

Let us consider that God calls for repentance before He sends out His judgments. We are in times when He has sent locusts and is sending plagues, but not His full wrath. He is giving us time to repent. Generation "ZION," please pray 2 Chronicles 7:13-16. The condition of humbling oneself, praying, seeking God's face, repenting, and turning our faces towards God so that He will come in and stop His wrath.

He wants to forgive us during these wicked times. Abba is crying out for His remnant to:

"WAKEUP! SOUND THE ALARM! WATCH ME DO AS I SAY! REPENT so that I can heal your land. Proclaim the prayer, sing it to Me. I do not enjoy this, but I love those I have chosen. Choose Me, choose life. Choose My ways. Give up anything contrary to My ways. Love righteousness. Love the Cross that gives you My righteousness!" says the Lord. Pray this prayer of repentance Generation "Zion."

Intercession Prayer for Generation Zion

If I shut up the sky so that there is no rain, or if I command the locust to devour the land, or if I send pestilence among my people;if my people, who are called by my name, will humble themselves, pray, seek my face, and turn from their wicked ways, then I will hear from heaven, will forgive their sin, and will heal their land. Now my eyes will be open and my ears attentive to prayer that is made in this place. For now I have chosen and made this house holy, that my name may be there forever; and my eyes and my heart will be there perpetually (2 Chr. 7:13-16).

ADDENDUM

This third edition revises certain Scripture references. Typographical and formatting errors.

ENDNOTES

1 John C. Hagee, *Prophecy Study Bible* (Nashville, TN.: Thomas Nelson Publishers, 1997), p. 1388.

2 http://dictionary.reference.com/search?q=debauchery *Webster's Revised Unabridged Dictionary, 1996, 1998 MICRA, Inc.*

3 The skeletal 4 point outline of Hypocrites is from John C. Hagee, *Prophecy Study Bible*, Evidences – Don't Blame Jesus for Hypocrites in the Church section – Hypocrites Do Not Follow Jesus (Nashville, TN.: Thomas Nelson Publishers, 1997), p. 1422.

4 Ibid, p. 1422.

5 Ibid, p. 1422.

6 Ibid, p. 1422.

7 Ché Ahn, *Into the Fire* (Ventura, California: Renew Books A Division of Gospel Light, 1998), p. 19 with ref. John Arnott, *The Father's Blessing* (Lake Mary, Fla.: Creation House, 1995), p. 29.

8 http://dictionary.reference.com/search?q=revolution *The American Heritage® Dictionary of the English Language, Fourth Edition. 2000 by Houghton Mifflin Company. Published by Houghton Mifflin Company. All rights reserved.*

9 Ché Ahn, *Into the Fire* (Ventura, California: Renew Books A Division of Gospel Light, 1998), p. 19.

10 Joseph Jacobs and Judah David Eisenstein, Temple, Administration and Service of, *Jewish Encyclopedia*, 1906, vol. 12, p. 81 (https://www.jewishencyclopedia.com/articles/14303-temple-administration-and-service) accessed March 29, 2021.

[11] Charles J. Cipiel, *REVOLUTION NOW!*, BY LIFE OR BY DEATH, (IN THE MEANTIME MUSIC), recorded at the Fire School of Ministry, Concord, NC, 2000.

[12] Mike Bickle, Library Forerunner School of Ministry, *STUDIES IN THE BEAUTY OF GOD The Emerald Rainbow: The God of Tender Mercy (Rev 4:3) Section I. THE GOD OF THE EMERALD RAINBOW notes on 4 Aug 2006.*

[13] Mike Bickle, Library Forerunner School of Ministry, *STUDIES IN THE BEAUTY OF GOD The Emerald Rainbow: The God of Tender Mercy (Rev 4:3) Section II. ALL OF GOD'S WORKS ARE SURROUNDED WITH MERCY* notes on 4 Aug 2006.

[14] Mike Bickle, Library International House of Prayer University, *Growing in Prayer (Part 2) Session 8 Praying Before God's Throne: The Perfection of Beauty II The Beauty of God's Person-How God Looks, Feels, and Acts (Rev 4:3) Section B Jasper Stone* notes on 1 May 2015.

[15] Mike Bickle, Library International House of Prayer University, *Growing in Prayer (Part 2) Session 8 Praying Before God's Throne: The Perfection of Beauty II The Beauty of God's Person-How God Looks, Feels, and Acts (Rev 4:3) Section D An emerald rainbow* notes on 1 May 2015.

[16] http://scienceline.ucsb.edu/getkey.php?key=5621 *Why is blue hotter than purple?,* (University of California Santa Barbara Science Line Question Date November 3, 2016).

[17] Melissa Tumino, *THE ULTIMATE GUIDE TO THE COLORS IN THE BIBLE*, (Thinkaboutsuchthings.com 2020), p. 24.

[18] Ibid, p. 42.

[19] Ibid, p. 26.

[20] Ibid, p. 26.

[21] Ibid, p. 14.

[22] Ibid, p. 14.

23 Ibid, p. 19.

24 Ibid, p. 27.

25 Ibid, p. 29.

26 Ibid.

27 Dirk Reien, *The Correlation between Structure and Color of Iron Oxide-type Solids, Sustainable Pigments with Gentle Hues*, (J. Inorganic and Gen. Chem. Abstract (https://doi.org/10.1002/zaac.201400384) Vol. 640, Iss. 14, Hoboken, NJ: John Wiley & Sons, Inc., 2014).

28 Melissa Tumino, Ibid, p. 29.

29 Ibid, p.31.

30 Ibid.

31 Ibid, pp.30-31.

32 Ibid p.32.

33 Ibid, p.34.

34 Ibid, pp.34-35.

35 Ibid, p.22.

36 http://gospelthroughart.canalblog.com/archives/2016/10/17/34449242.html, THE RAINBOW AND COLORS OF GOD, October 17, 2016.

37 Melissa Tumino, Ibid, pp. 36-37.

38 AoM Team, *How to Gird Up Your Loins: An Illustrated Guide*, 2021 (https://www.artofmanliness.com/skills/manly-know-how/how-to-gird-up-your-loins-an-illustrated-guide), accessed July 13, 2022.

39 Rich Robinson, *The Tallit and Tzitzit*, https://jewsforjesus.org/publications/newsletter/newsletter-sep-1993/the-tallit-and-tzitzit, (January 1, 1994).

40 Rich Robinson, Ibid.

[41] David Jeremiah, *Spiritual Warfare Terms of Engagement Study Guide*, (San Diego, California: Turning Point with David Jeremiah, 2020), p. 115.

[43] Ibid., pg. 75.

[44] David Jeremiah, *Spiritual Warfare Terms of Engagement Study Guide*, (San Diego, California: Turning Point with David Jeremiah, 2020), pg. 120.

[45] Ibid., p. 74.

[46] Stu Weber, *Spirit Warriors*, (Sisters, Oregon: Multnomah Publishers, 2001), p. 172.

[47] Jim W. Goll, *The Lost Art of Intercession: Restoring the Power and Passion of the Watch of the Lord*, (Shippensburg, Pennsylvania: Revival Press an imprint of Destiny Image® Publishers, Inc., 1997), pg. 16-17.

[48] Ibid., pg. 8.

[49] Ibid., pg. 17-18.

[50] Ibid., pp. 17-18.

[51] Ibid., pg. 20.

[52] Jim W. Goll, *The Lost Art of Intercession: Restoring the Power and Passion of the Watch of the Lord*, (Shippensburg, Pennsylvania: Revival Press an imprint of Destiny Image® Publishers, Inc., 1997), pp. 116-117.

[53] blueletterbible.org, *tef-il-law*, https://www.blueletterbible.org/lexicon/h8605/kjv/wlc/0-1/, accessed October 4, 2021.

[54] ibid. *tef-il-law*

[55] Jim W. Goll, *The Lost Art of Intercession: Restoring the Power and Passion of the Watch of the Lord*, (Shippensburg, Pennsylvania: Revival Press an imprint of Destiny Image® Publishers, Inc., 1997), pg. 93.

[56] Ibid., pg. 39.

[57] blueletterbible.org, *pros-yoo-khay'*, https://www.blueletterbible.org/lexicon/g4335/kjv/lxx/0-2/#lexResults, accessed October 4, 2021.

[58] bluletterbible.org, *pros-yoo'-khom-ahee*, https://www.blueletterbible.org/lexicon/g4336/kjv/tr/0-1, accessed October 4, 2021.

[59] bluletterbible.org, *leg'-o*, https://www.blueletterbible.org/lexicon/g3004/kjv/mgnt/0-1/#lexResults, accessed October 4, 2021.

BIBLIOGRAPHY

Books

Ché Ahn, *Into the Fire* (Ventura, California: Renew Books A Division of Gospel Light, 1998)

Jim W. Goll, *The Lost Art of Intercession: Restoring the Power and Passion of the Watch of the Lord*, (Shippensburg, Pennsylvania: Revival Press an imprint of Destiny Image® Publishers, Inc., 1997)

John C. Hagee, *Prophecy Study Bible* (Nashville, TN.: Thomas Nelson Publishers, 1997)

David Jeremiah, *Spiritual Warfare Terms of Engagement Study Guide*, (San Diego, California: Turning Point with David Jeremiah, 2020)

Melissa Tumino, *THE ULTIMATE GUIDE TO THE COLORS IN THE BIBLE*, (Thinkaboutsuchthings.com 2020)

Stu Weber, *Spirit Warriors*, (Sisters, Oregon: Multnomah Publishers, 2001)

Articles/Study Notes/Websites

Art of Manliness Team, *How to Gird Up Your Loins: An Illustrated Guide*, 2021 (https://www.artofmanliness.com/skills/manly-know-how/how-to-gird-up-your-loins-an-illustrated-guide)

Mike Bickle, Library International House of Prayer University, *Growing in Prayer (Part 2) Session 8 Praying Before God's Throne: The Perfection of Beauty II The Beauty of God's Person-How God Looks, Feels, and Acts (Rev 4:3)*

Mike Bickle, Library Forerunner School of Ministry, *STUDIES IN THE BEAUTY OF GOD The Emerald Rainbow: The God of Tender Mercy (Rev 4:3)*

Joseph Jacobs and Judah David Eisenstein, Temple, Administration and Service of, *Jewish Encyclopedia*, 1906, vol. 12, p. 81 (https://www.jewishencyclopedia.com/articles/14303-temple-administration-and-service)

Dirk Reien, *The Correlation between Structure and Color of Iron Oxide-type Solids, Sustainable Pigments with Gentle Hues*, (J. Inorganic and Gen. Chem. Abstract (https://doi.org/10.1002/zaac.201400384) Vol. 640, Iss. 14, Hoboken, NJ: John Wiley & Sons, Inc., 2014)

Rich Robinson, *The Tallit and Tzitzit*, https://jewsforjesus.org/publications/newsletter/newsletter-sep-1993/the-tallit-and-tzitzit, (January 1, 1994).

http://dictionary.reference.com/search?q=debauchery *Webster's Revised Unabridged Dictionary, 1996, 1998 MICRA, Inc.*

http://dictionary.reference.com/search?q=revolution *The American Heritage® Dictionary of the English Language, Fourth Edition. 2000 by Houghton Mifflin Company. Published by Houghton Mifflin Company. All rights reserved*

http://gospelthroughart.canalblog.com/archives/2016/10/17/34449242.html, THE RAINBOW AND COLORS OF GOD, October 17, 2016

http://scienceline.ucsb.edu/getkey.php?key=5621 *Why is blue hotter than purple?*, (University of California Santa Barbara Science Line Question Date November 3, 2016)

<u>Songs</u>

Charles J. Cipiel, *REVOLUTION NOW!*, BY LIFE OR BY DEATH, (IN THE MEANTIME MUSIC), recorded at the Fire School of Ministry, Concord, NC, 2000

Don't miss out!

Visit the website below and you can sign up to receive emails whenever Dennis Grimes publishes a new book. There's no charge and no obligation.

https://books2read.com/r/B-A-KJUCB-XHSWC

Connecting independent readers to independent writers.

Also by Dennis Grimes

Generation Zion
Generation Zion
The Melchizedek Priesthood Garments
The Melchizedek Priesthood Robes

About the Author

Dennis Grimes resides in Paris, TX with his wife Faith and two children. He is a Prayer Shepherd. Besides being a Prayer Shepherd, he is an itinerant minister at Teen Blaze/First Youth Nations in Southern California and Believers Ministry International. His passion for prayer and revival is sparked to see a multigenerational movement of God that will help bring forth the Global End-Time Harvest and End-Time Revival.